MAMMOTH MTN.
11,053'

MAMMOTH MTN.
SKI AREA

BRIDGEPORT

MINARET ROAD

LEE VINING

MONO LAKE

ANSEL
ADAMS
WILDERNESS

JUNE MTN.

CRESTVIEW

CAPE MENDOCINO

MAMMOTH LAKES

203

LAKE
CROWLEY

SACRAMENTO

395

TOMS PLACE

SAN FRANCISCO

OWENS RIVER

BISHOP

SAN JOSE

MONTEREY
BAY

SIERRA NEVADA

SAN JOAQUIN VALLEY

BAKERSFIELD

MT WHITNEY
14,495'

SANTA
BARBARA

LOS ANGELES

14

CHANNEL ISLANDS

SAN DIEGO

Mammoth
the sierra legend

BY MARTIN FORSTENZER

MOUNTAIN SPORTS PRESS

BOULDER, COLORADO USA

OWENS VALLEY

BIG PINE

INDEPENDENCE

LONE PINE

395

DEATH VALLEY

NEVADA

ARIZ

14

MOJAVE DESERT

395

AN BERNARDINO

SALTON SEA

MEXICO

Mammoth: The Sierra Legend

Published by Mountain Sports Press

Distributed to the book trade by:
PUBLISHERS GROUP WEST

Bill Grout, *Editor-in-Chief*
Michelle Klammer Schrantz, *Art Director*
Alan Stark, *Associate Publisher*
Scott Kronberg, *Photo Editor & Associate Art Director*
Chris Salt, *Production Manager*
Andy Hawk, *Account Manager*

ISBN 0-9717748-0-3
Library of Congress Cataloging-in-Publiscation Data applied for.

Printed in Canada by Friesens Corporation

Prepress by Westphal West, Boulder, Colorado

Cover photo: Skier Shane Chandlee descends Dos Pasos on the back
side of Mammoth Mountain near chair 14.

MOUNTAIN SPORTS PRESS

A subsidiary of:
TIME4MEDIA

929 Pearl Street, Suite 200
Boulder, CO 80302
303-448-7617

For my mother, Estelle

CONTENTS

preface   By Warren Miller

first met Dave McCoy when I raced against him in the Far West Ski Association championships in 1948, a race that Dave won and I placed a distant second.

Our paths didn't cross again until Thanksgiving weekend of 1950 in the parking lot midway between the town of Mammoth Lakes and Dave's tiny new base lodge at the foot of Mammoth Mountain. I had driven up from Los Angeles in my 1949 Chevy panel delivery truck. In those days it was an eight- or nine-hour drive on a two-lane road. Not a single mile of freeway existed anywhere.

But the long drive was worth it, because Mammoth was one of only two places in the country where you could count on good snow for Thanksgiving (Alta, Utah, was the other). Dave had built two rope tows and a 400-square-foot base lodge. He even had different "rest rooms" for men and women that consisted of a pair of holes dug in the snow with some semblance of a building around them and more ventilation than you cared to have.

That morning I pulled up in front of the Mammoth Tavern and Lodge at 3:00 a.m., climbed into my army surplus sleeping bag in the back of the panel truck and slept soundly until the car parked next to me started up about 6:00 a.m. (I quickly realized that the guy starting his car that early must know something about skiing at Mammoth that I didn't.) I sat up in bed, still wrapped in my sleeping bag, and lit my Coleman stove so I could melt the ice in the pot I had filled with water the night before. By the time it thawed out, the inside of the truck was warm enough to melt the frost off the ceiling, so I started dressing while my oatmeal was cooking.

After breakfast I drove to the end of the plowed road where, even at that hour, there were already half a dozen other cars parked, their occupants in various stages of cooking breakfast, getting dressed for skiing, waxing skis, or commiserating about how late they had got to Mammoth the night before. All of us were thankful it would be a blue-sky day, just as soon as the sun came up.

The word in the parking lot was, "Dave McCoy has gone in on the Weasel to pack the road and warm up the rope-tow engine. He should be back by 7:30 or 8:00."

Sure enough, Dave was back at 7:45. He spun the Weasel around and paused long enough for half a dozen ladies to climb in. The rest of us, with our lunches in our rucksacks, hung onto ropes that trailed out behind the Weasel while Dave towed us the four or five miles into his ski area.

At the base lodge, I paid Dave's wife Roma $2.50 for my lift ticket and, clutching my rope-tow gripper, began my first day of the season on Mammoth Mountain. Riding a rope tow all day long was a memorable but exhausting experience. By the end of the day every muscle, tendon and fiber in my body was stretched to the breaking point. A lot of people claimed that after a couple of weekends of hanging onto Dave McCoy's rope tows, your right arm would be one inch longer than your left.

Since 1950 I have managed to ski at Mammoth almost every winter, and Mammoth always occupied a prominent position in my ski films. When I would arrive with my film crew, Dave would always have a new chairlift, a new method of snow grooming or a new idea to prove the old saying, "Lead the parade, join in behind, or sit and watch it go by." Dave always led the parade, and each winter I'd be amazed at what he and his band of faithful employees managed to build. He built one of the world's first two-stage gondolas to the top of the mountain at over 11,000 feet. You could get off at midway if you were timid, or go for greatness to the summit. But from either starting point you could go home and tell your friends, "I skied the gondola."

The good old days at Mammoth have continued uninterrupted since my first trip there. The road is still 300 miles from downtown Los Angeles, but today it is a four-lane freeway almost every mile of the way. The town has grown from the six full-time residents to a population of 6,500 today. And over the years, Dave McCoy has been the driving force behind almost everything that has happened at Mammoth. He even helped build the first school, the hospital, the water district and now the community college.

At age 87 Dave McCoy still rides a mountain bike, still roars around on a motorcycle, and still goes to work in his corner office in the Mammoth Base Lodge. Unlike most other resort developers who wind up in the real estate business, Dave told me years ago that he didn't want to buy up a lot of land and build beds for the skiers. "I don't want to be in competition with the small lodge owners. I just want to build ski lifts and develop more skiing so more people can finish the day with a smile."

As big as Mammoth Mountain is, Dave McCoy is bigger. ✤

Woolly and Warren.

Previous page: The largest freshwater lake in the region, Crowley Lake mirrors the Eastern Sierra mountains. Left to right, beginning at the center of the photo: Mount Morgan, McGee Mountain, Mount Morrison and Laurel Mountain. Above: The Minarets rise above an alpine lake in the Ansel Adams Wilderness.

c h a p t e r   1

The Untamed Land

When *San Francisco Evening Post* correspondent James W.A. Wright came to the Eastern Sierra in 1879 to write about the region's gold miners, he couldn't believe his eyes. Spread out before him were "all elements of the sublime, immense, picturesque, curious, weird, and varied in forms, colors, and startling contrasts…of mountain, valley and lake scenery."

Captivated by the beauty, drama and sheer primordial outlandishness of the terrain surrounding the newly established town of Mammoth City, California, he returned to explore and map sections of the range. Today, first-time visitors to the Eastern Sierra can find themselves just as surprised and exhilarated by the grand and rugged landscape.

The Sierra Nevada's soaring peaks stretch northward almost 400 miles, from Southern California's Mojave Desert to the state's northeastern volcanic tablelands. Wright, who eventually gave his name to a group of wilderness lakes and a creek near Mount Whitney, was enthralled by the range's eastern slope partly because it was so startlingly different from what he had already seen on the western side. On its western slope, leafy, river-laced foothills climb slowly up from the Central Valley to the high cliffs of the Sierra Crest, but on the eastern side, the Sierra's flanks turn into an escarpment—a granite wall that plunges down to the arid Great Basin.

The Eastern Sierra is a land of wild extremes. The 14,495-foot, ice-topped Mount Whitney, the highest peak in the Lower 48, stands just dozens of miles from the lowest ground in North America at Badwater (282 feet below sea level) in blistering Death Valley, where temperatures can top 130 degrees. The stormy mountains covered with Jeffrey and lodgepole pines, and plaited with miles of rushing streams, tower over the stark, dusty Owens Valley, a skip away from another valley of high sand dunes. Gnarled bristlecone pines, the oldest living things on earth—dating back as far as 4,600 years—stand battered by gale winds on top of the nearby White Mountains.

Mammoth Mountain rises some 50 miles to the northwest, broad, humpbacked and audacious. It dominates the landscape, jutting from the range and displaying its full span as a lure to travelers who approach from the south through the Owens and Long valleys.

Since the northern stretch of the range is considered a part of the Lake Tahoe region, the name Eastern Sierra has come to designate the southern section lying in two spacious counties that sprawl

Ancient glaciers scoured and sculpted the huge granite formations that make up the Eastern Sierra Nevada.

to the Nevada border, Inyo and Mono. Unlike the open western flank, the sparsely populated eastern slope has always been troublesome to reach from most of California throughout the year, and virtually cut off in winter when almost all roads over the range are closed by snow. It does remain accessible from Southern California by way of U.S. 395 through the high desert, and the Eastern Sierra has become the favorite vacationland of travelers from Los Angeles, San Diego and other Southland cities.

For all its icy stillness, the Sierra Nevada was born in fiery cataclysm. A few hundred million years ago, molten rock surged up from beneath the earth's surface. Some of it solidified into volcanic rock; other parts stayed buried to crystallize into immense mounds of granite. Glaciers followed, stripping off the volcanic layers, exposing the granite and sculpting it into the colossal formations that wall in the valley floors.

An earth-shattering eruption 760,000 years ago in Long Valley, just southeast of where the town of Mammoth Lakes stands now, threw out a massive 150 cubic miles of volcanic debris, blackening the skies and blanketing the area of several downwind states with thick layers of ash. The blast was 2,000 times greater than the eruption of Mount St. Helens, enough to transform the region's climate and hurl ash so violently upward that some of it has been found in Nebraska and Kansas. That explosion left behind a 10- by 20-mile volcanic basin called the Long Valley Caldera. Several hundred thousand years later, eruptions at the western edge of the caldera formed a group of pumice-covered domes that merged into one big monster of volcanic rock—Mammoth Mountain, more than four miles wide from east to west and 11,053 feet high.

Above: From the trailhead it's 6,000 vertical feet to the top of 14,495-foot Mount Whitney, the highest peak in the continental United States. Below: Basalt columns form the Devils Postpile.

Eastern Sierra dwellers have always had to live with seismic unrest. In 1872, a massive 8.0 magnitude earthquake—the largest ever to hit California—struck the town of Lone Pine 100 miles south of Mammoth, collapsing most of the town's buildings. Headlines in a local newspaper screamed, "HORRORS! APPALLING TIMES! EARTHQUAKES! AWFUL LOSS OF LIFE! 25 PERSONS

KILLED! HOUSES PROSTRATED! LONE PINE! ITS TERRIBLE CONDITION! MOST HEART-RENDING SCENES!" A 12-mile crack opened, sinking the land alongside of it more than a dozen feet. At least one horse and one ox were swallowed whole, and the course of the Owens River reversed to flow north instead of south. Periods of temblors have followed. In the 1980s, the region between Lone Pine and Mono Lake was socked by a series of moderate 5.0 to 6.0 magnitude earthquakes. They jangled people's nerves more than they caused damage or injury, especially one post-midnight quake that struck the Owens Valley town of Bishop and roared like a locomotive from hell.

Around that same time, the Long Valley Caldera started to bulge mysteriously, rising about two feet over the past few decades. That swelling led scientists to speculate about possible tremors to come, or even a volcanic eruption in the caldera. Some Mammoth residents were concerned about those warnings, while others brushed them off with "Shake and Bake" jokes. The truth is that geologists aren't able to make precise long-range predictions, except to say that the caldera is just as likely to erupt several hundred years from now as next year. Mammothites can live with those odds.

Eastern Sierra geologic formations and oddities are so diverse and accessible that universities from around the country bring geology classes to study them on field trips. A tour of the region takes you past craters, cinder cones and obsidian domes, earthquake faults and fumaroles. Devils Postpile National Monument on Mammoth's western flank is a lava flow that cracked into a gigantic heap of hexagonal rods. Ancient Mono Lake 25 miles north of Mammoth is twice as salty as seawater and dotted with oddly shaped tufa towers that rise above its surface. Small glaciers still cover parts of the eastern slope, remnants of the massive ice sheets that shaped the mountains and carved basins like the one that holds the gemlike chain of lakes at the foot of Mammoth Mountain. If the area's volcanism has upset some locals, it has at least provided them with some popular bathing spots. The natural bathing pools at the Whitmore Hot Springs in Long Valley, which average around 80 degrees Fahrenheit, have long been a favorite après-ski soak, and those who cross-country ski to Hot Creek not far away are rewarded with a steaming dip.

Mammoth Mountain ski resort offers a lengthy season because heavy snows hammer it throughout the winter and well into spring, piling up considerably higher than they do in the surrounding area. The reason is geography. The High Sierra blocks clouds that drive in from the Pacific, forcing them upward and wringing out their moisture. The gradual western slope can receive eight to 10 times as much precipitation as areas on the eastern side. But Mammoth Mountain happens to stand directly opposite Mammoth Pass, a wide, low spot in the range. Storms that roll up from

Mammoth Mountain, February, 1927, long before lifts or trails.

the flat Central Valley along a deep canyon incised by the middle fork of the San Joaquin River are funneled over the low pass, where they slam directly into the only obstacle in their path, Mammoth Mountain. There, they drop their snowy payload. It can snow on the highest reaches of the mountain in any month of the year, even August. Still, storms tend to pass quickly, leaving the mountain bathed in sunshine about 80 percent of the year. "This isn't the Pacific Northwest, where the clouds hang in the mountains," says Clifford Mann, Mammoth's director of mountain maintenance and resident weather expert. "The storms roll through here and snow and blow like hell, and when they disappear, they're gone and we get crystal blue."

Historically, extremes of climate and quirks of geography have made the Eastern Sierra a harsh, austere land where people had to be tough and resourceful to survive. The band of Paiute Indians that lived along the shores of Mono Lake, where saline waters support no life except tiny brine shrimp and brine flies, were called the Kuzedika, or "fly eaters." They sun-dried the flies' small

white pupae and depended on them as a staple food, along with pine nuts, caterpillars, lizards and occasional larger game.

The first U.S. expedition into the Owens Valley from what is now northern Nevada, in 1845, led by explorer John C. Frémont with legendary outdoorsman Kit Carson as guide, was forced to eat its own horses and pack animals because its members couldn't find any game to shoot or fish to catch. Or, as Frémont himself vividly put it, "We had tonight an extraordinary dinner—pea soup, mule and dog."

After the Paiutes and Shoshones, the Eastern Sierra was settled by miners who trickled over from the west side of the range after the 1849 gold rush. The trickle changed to a deluge 10 years later when prospectors discovered gold in a wash near Mono Lake, the same year that miners digging east of Lake Tahoe struck the sensational Comstock Lode, which ultimately yielded $700 million in ore. Five thousand men swiftly alighted in mining towns named Bodie and Aurora that shot up north of Mono Lake. Mono County was formally created a few years later in response to the population boom, with Aurora named its county seat. Officials were very red-faced when a surveying party discovered that Aurora actually sat on the wrong side of the California border in what is now Nevada. They hastily scrambled to rename the town of Bridgeport the new county seat, which it is still, despite concerted attempts a century later by residents of Mammoth Lakes to move it to their ski resort town.

While prospectors were searching for gold in northern Mono County, tales rapidly spread through the gold fields about a wide ledge of reddish lava, called "cement," studded with staggeringly large nuggets of gold. They said this ledge was found about eight miles north of Pumice Mountain—then the name of Mammoth Mountain.

"Lumps of virgin gold were as thick in it as raisins in a slice of fruit cake," Mark Twain wrote about the Lost Cement Mine, as it came to be known, in his book *Roughing It*. In a

longer version of the story written by the journalist Wright, two men hiking across the Sierra in 1857 sat down to rest in the area "somewhere on the headwaters of the Owens River" and noticed the shelf of red cement. They took a chunk to be assayed and found that it was in fact heavily laden with gold. Afterward, the pair and a succession of other men attempted to mine the ledge, but were foiled by Indian attack, terminal illness, encroaching rivals and a murderous feud between partners. Since then, countless prospectors have spent many fruitless months trying to find the rich deposit, and people still look for it today, even though no one really knows for sure whether the story was true or a wholly invented fable.

True or not, the story led to the creation of the town of Mammoth Lakes. In the 1870s, a group of prospectors out searching

Ancient Indians carved petroglyphs into this rock on the floor of the Owens Valley.

MYSTERIOUS MONO LAKE

Beside the town of Lee Vining, at the bottom of the steep grade that drops from the western edge of Yosemite National Park, lies a strange lake of enigmatic beauty. Sometimes shrouded in thick mist, 730,000-year-old Mono Lake stretches for 14 miles between the Sierra mountains and the Nevada border, a primeval oval with two volcanic islands poking up at its center. Sightseers stop to gaze across its waters by the hundreds of thousands each year, and scores of professional photographers are drawn to shoot photos of the pink- and purple-hued sunsets that reflect off its mirror surface, or of the tufa towers that rise high above it.

Mono Lake is a remnant of a much larger Ice Age body of water that geologists call Lake Russell, which once extended twice as far across the basin. When it dried into what is now Mono Lake, it left no outlet, and it became increasingly saline as it shrank—and more alkaline than ammonia. No fish can live in Mono Lake—in fact, nothing at all lives in the lake except for tiny brine shrimp and the larvae of

Before legal victories by the Mono Lake Committee gave it protection, the lake was in danger of becoming a dead pool.

brine flies. However, Mono is part of an ancient system of lakes that migratory birds have been using as stopovers for thousands of years, and millions of grebes, phalaropes and other water birds stop and feed at the lake. Also gobbling the brine shrimp and flies are thousands of California gulls, which used an island in the lake as a major rookery.

Between 1941 and 1982, the Los Angeles Department of Water and Power diverted four of Mono Lake's five major feeder streams, causing the lake's level to drop by 45 feet. The agency, which owns water rights throughout Mono County and the Owens Valley to the south, channeled the stream water to the Southern California metropolis for drinking water. As its level dropped, the lake was in danger of becoming a dead pool, so saline that it would have been unable to support even brine shrimp or flies, essentially ruining it as wildlife habitat.

In 1978, David Gaines, a local naturalist who had grown concerned about the fate of the gull rookery, got together with a few other people and formed a group called the Mono Lake

Limestone tufa towers that stand above its surface are part of the lake's enigmatic look.

Committee to try to protect the lake. In what was often called a "David and Goliath" struggle, the small organization battled the city of Los Angeles for years, filing numerous court actions and turning the fight to protect Mono Lake into an international cause célèbre. *Save Mono Lake* bumper stickers were affixed to pickups and sedans not only in Mammoth and Bishop, but also in cities throughout California and across the country.

In the end, the little group was victorious. In 1994, the state limited water diversions and mandated that the lake's surface be raised 17 feet during the next 20 years and maintained at a healthy 6,392 feet above sea level. The lake is today the central attraction of the Mono Basin National Forest Scenic Area, and a visitor center was built on its western side near Highway 395. Unfortunately, David Gaines, the passionate advocate for the lake, was killed in a car accident not far from its shores in 1988, and he never saw the final success of his dogged effort to save it.

for the fabulous Lost Cement Mine instead struck a rich, nonfictional gold deposit on Mineral Hill, near the current location of the town. Other miners soon followed to stake dozens of claims in the area. One group of five claims was purchased by a prominent mining investor named General George S. Dodge, who incorporated them as the Mammoth Mining Company. Pumice Mountain was renamed Mammoth Mountain, and the town of Mammoth City, with a population that eventually reached more than 2,500 miners, sprouted at its base. Workers laid in a new supply road to Bishop that later became the route of U.S. Highway 395, which is today the main artery running through the Eastern Sierra. The only artery, in fact.

The miners soon learned about the 8,000-foot-high town's propensity for attracting snow. During the winter of 1879–80, snowfall came late to Mammoth City, but December storms then pounded it nonstop for 18 days. By season's end, 28 feet of snow had dumped on the mountain town. Residents were forced to cut a warren of snow tunnels to allow them to make their way through the town, and businesses hacked long rows of

The Mammoth Mining Company's stamp mill was shut down shortly after it began operating in the late 1870s.

snow steps down to their front doors. Some snowbound miners tried traversing the snowy hills around Mammoth on skis, using barrel staves or long, flat boards carved out of oak. They had heard about the exploits of an immigrant from Telemark, Norway, named John "Snowshoe" Thompson, who had introduced skiing to the Sierra 20 years earlier. A prospector who had given up on dreams of striking it rich in the gold fields, Thompson took a job carrying the U.S. mail over the Sierra from Genoa, Nevada, to Placerville, California. Thompson became a Sierra legend for unfailingly hauling the mail dozens of miles a day and crossing its dangerous high passes through snowstorms, gale winds and bitter cold.

At least $200,000 in gold ore was found at Mammoth, but it wasn't enough to keep the town going. Its mill was shut down for good shortly after it was built, and after the brutal winter of 1879–80, miners took off in droves for places with gentler climates.

Finally, only a handful of residents remained. Some of the miners stayed on to start cattle ranches or run sheep in the mountains, and ranching grew to become the backbone of the local economy.

While Mammoth City had generally been a law-abiding town, that wasn't true of Bodie and Aurora, a few dozen miles to the north. They were notorious for their lawlessness and debauchery. One street in Bodie was lined with brothels and dance halls, while another supported nearly 50 saloons. According to Roger McGrath's book *Gunfighters, Highwaymen and Vigilantes: Violence on the Frontier*, some of Bodie's saloons served home-brewed whisky, said to be made from "old boots, scraps of iron, snow-slides and climate, and it only takes a couple of 'snorts' to craze a man of ordinary brainpower."

Mining companies employed hired guns to intimidate rival outfits, outlaws held up stagecoaches, and gunfighters occasionally shot each other down in the streets in personal disputes or fights over women. It didn't always take that much to touch off a brawl. One Bodie miner was shot dead in the town's Dividend Saloon in a fight with a professional gambler over an accidentally ripped jacket. Lee Vining of Aurora was among the first prospectors in the area, and he stayed on to build a sawmill on one of the creeks feeding Mono Lake. He was also killed in a saloon fight, apparently shooting himself in the groin when he tried to pull his gun out of his pants. Despite his unlucky end, or maybe because of it, the creek and the town on the lakeshore still carry his name.

The "Bad Man from Bodie" became an infamous legend. In one account, a town desperado stood up on a saloon billiard table and announced, "Here I am again, a mile wide and all wool. I weigh a ton and when I walk the earth shakes. I'm a sandstorm mixed with a whirlwind. I'm bad from the bottom up and clear grit plumb through. I'm chief of Murdertown, and I'm dry. Whose treat is it? Don't all speak at once, or I'll turn loose and scatter death and destruction full bent for the next election."

Preserved buildings from the late 1800s still stand in the ghost town of Bodie, a mining camp notorious for its lawlessness.

Soon after Mammoth faded as a mining town, it was reborn as a sleepy little summer resort. Sometime around the turn of the century in an idyllic meadow near Mammoth Creek, Charles F. Wildasinn started the first summer lodge, a modest little hotel with a small store nearby. A number of other hotels followed, including Tamarack Lodge, built of logs and wood planks in the mid 1920s and featuring a big stone fireplace in the lobby. Perched on the shore of picturesque Twin Lakes on the backside of Mammoth Mountain, the well-preserved lodge is one of the few original Mammoth inns still entertaining guests.

Most of the lodge owners stayed only during the summer, vacating before the heavy winter snows cut the town off from the

THE GHOSTS OF BODIE

The 19th-century mining town of Bodie still stands in the high-desert sagebrush north of Mono Lake. Deer and antelope play nearby, and discouraging words are seldom heard because no one lives here anymore. All of the residents emptied out after the uproarious town's boom days ended, but the ghost town was turned into a California state historic park. It's one of the best preserved of any of the West's ghost towns, kept in a state of "arrested decay" since it was declared a historic site in 1962.

"That means that we don't allow buildings to fall over anymore than they had by 1962," says Carrie Rasmussen, who works as an aide at the park. They prop up buildings from the inside and outside, and sometimes replace roofs or foundations, using original materials as much as possible. The 170 houses and buildings scattered over hundreds of acres in the park are built mostly of bare wood—wind and weather stripped the paint off long ago. Those structures actually represent less than five percent of the original

Wooden skis that once provided winter
transportation for miners.

town. Most of Bodie, which once was made up of around 2,000 buildings, burned in a series of fires.

The Methodist church is still standing, and so are the post office and the once-busy town jail. The bank burned down, but its brick vault remains erect. The Standard Mine and Mill, which yielded nearly $15 million in bullion before it shut down, still stands overlooking the town from Bodie Bluff. The buildings retain many of their original furnishings: Tables, chairs and dressers remain in their old positions, pictures hang on the walls and kitchen utensils still lie on tabletops. Shops display goods in their windows, and cues still lie on the billiard table in one of the old hotels. Over 200,000 visitors a year wander through the ghost town, which has been kept almost completely uncommercialized. It offers no services, not even so much as a snack bar, except for the Bodie Museum housed inside the old Miner's Union Hall, where at least one notorious gun battle took place. The museum is filled with artifacts from the town: photograph

Above and right: Although 170 houses and buildings remain standing in Bodie, most of the town burned in a series of fires.

albums, ladies' fancy hats, children's toys, dinner plates and assorted other items. Bodie retains a strange, intangible presence, and visitors walking over its dirt streets and raised wooden sidewalks often say that they are struck by an eerie, indefinable sensation. It could be because the buildings remain in such good condition, and the belongings of Bodie's long-gone residents remain inside their old houses, as if they might be coming back. ✺

Above: Tamarack Lodge, built in the 1920s, was among the first summer resorts to open at Mammoth. Below: Today's Tamarack Lodge still entertains guests throughout the year.

highway. While a hearty few remained during those months, other lodge owners hired adventurous caretakers to stay on to shovel snow off the rooftops and do other maintenance. Some years, the town had as few as six year-round residents. One of them was Tex Cushion, a tough French Canadian who came to Mammoth with his wife, Ruth, in the winter of 1927. The sawed-off, dark-haired Cushion, a former bootlegger during Prohibition, changed his name from Couchane and adopted the name Tex because he liked its cowboy sound. He learned to telemark from a Swiss immigrant doctor from Southern California named H. F. Rey, who was drawn to Mammoth because it reminded him of his old home near the Alps. Cushion became a seminal figure in the early days of Eastern Sierra skiing.

The view from Tamarack Lodge stretches across beautiful Twin Lakes to the backcountry beyond.

Above, left: French Canadian Tex Cushion used his dog teams to deliver mail and supplies. Sometimes he rescued stranded travelers. Above, right: Friends of Tex Cushion sit outside his Mammoth cabin, which he dubbed the Winter Patrol Station.

Cushion named his cabin the Winter Patrol Station, and he and his wife often hosted those rugged folks who lived, worked or skied near the isolated village during its snowy off-season. He was best known for running a sled-dog team on a regular winter patrol, delivering mail, freight and supplies to the handful of nearby miners and other winter residents. He mushed the dogsled through white-out blizzards and over tall snow drifts, and occasionally was called upon to use his huskies to rescue people lost or stranded in the white wilderness.

In winter, a pair of skis or Cushion's dog sled were the only means of transportation available to Mammoth travelers.

One cold December, Cushion was on his way to the Minaret Mine deep in the Mammoth backcountry on the other side of the ice-covered San Joaquin River. Just as he approached the river's far shore, the ice broke apart and he and his dogs were plunged into the swirling, frigid water. Cushion managed to grab a branch and pull himself, the dogs and the attached sled out of the icy San Joaquin. He immediately stripped off his wet clothing and tended to his dogs' feet, knowing that they could be crippled by freezing. Finishing that, he wrapped himself in a bearskin rug and built a fire. They returned to his cabin two days later, safe if not entirely sound. Cushion sometimes took the dogs to Los Angeles to display them at the Automobile Club of Southern California Sports Show, and drew crowds when he raced his team up Figueroa Street. On occasion, movie crews hired him when they were shooting on location in the Mammoth area, using his teams for filming Yukon and other snowy tales.

Nan and Max Zischank were hired as winter caretakers at the Tamarack Lodge in 1935–36, which turned out to be the winter of one of the heaviest snowfalls on record. They kept their firewood stacked to the ceiling in one of their cabin bedrooms to keep it dry, and survived mostly on dried and canned food. The exception was a side of beef that they kept hanging frozen outside. When they needed a piece, the Zischanks hacked one off with a six-foot crosscut saw. Tex Cushion passed his knowledge of skiing on to the Zischanks, and Nan evolved into one of the Eastern Sierra's finest skiers and top racers. The couple later bought their own ski lodge in Long Valley near McGee Mountain, and named it Nan and Max's Long Valley Resort.

Above: Old Mammoth, with still-snowy Mammoth Mountain looming above it, was a sleepy summer resort in the early 1930s. By 1937, the town's businesses had to relocate closer to the new Highway 203, which bypassed the old town. Left: Swiss immigrant Dr. H.F. Rey of Oxnard skied to the lakes basin with his son. Rey, who helped introduce skiing technique to the Eastern Sierra, often came to his Mammoth cabin in winter.

Penney's Bakery stood alongside Mammoth Creek until its owners moved closer to the new highway and opened Penney's Tavern.

In 1937, to provide tourists with an easy auto route to the beautiful Mammoth Lakes basin, the state built the Lake Mary Road, or Highway 203, which branched off U.S. 395 but completely bypassed the town of Mammoth. The town's businesspeople were forced to abandon their shops, inns and cafes in the meadow and literally erect a new town alongside the new highway. Nora and Frank Penney had run a bakery and lunch spot famous for its double oatmeal cookies and bear claws in Old Mammoth, as the area near the Mammoth Creek meadow became known. In the new village, they decided to build a two-story lodge, bar and restaurant called Penney's Tavern at the corner of the new highway and Old Mammoth Road. It quickly became known as the wildest place in town, a summer hangout for people to go drinking, dancing to live bands and partying late into the night.

When skiing began to catch on, the Zischanks built a little rope tow on the hill behind their resort that they offered at no charge to their guests. The McGee Creek Lodge up the road changed its name to the McGee Creek Lodge and Ski Ranch, and began advertising an in-house ski instructor, a ski lift and rides on Cushion's dogsled. Those and a few other lodges along the highway were perfectly situated to provide steaks and hot buttered rum to the crowds of skiers that would soon be spending their days sporting in the nearby mountains. ✿

A snowy succession of Sierra peaks seen from Long Valley. McGee Mountain stands at right.

Previous page: Climbing Highway 395's Sherwin Grade toward Mammoth, motorists' eyes are drawn to Mount Tom (left) and the wall of Wheeler Crest looming to the West. Above: The Owens River starts north of Mammoth and ends near Lone Pine, where it is channeled into the L.A. aqueduct.

Early Eastern Sierra Winters

The drive through the Owens Valley to Mammoth wasn't an easy one when the first motorists started clattering up the old El Camino Sierra, the first highway to pass near the town. In the summer of 1927, when long-time Mammoth resident Adele Reed was about to set out on her first trip to the Eastern Sierra at the age of 25 in a heavily loaded 490 Chevrolet sedan, she heard nothing but ominous warnings from friends.

After hours of travel, she found out what they were talking about. "A burned-out main bearing meant camping under a big oak tree beside the road for two days and nights. As we headed north, the dire predictions did come true—rough roads, hot travel, blowouts and never-ending miles ahead," she wrote.

The dirt road through the valley followed old wagon routes and Indian trails, and it was dusty, deep-rutted and high-centered with only an occasional cafe or gas station oasis. It was worse in winter—a sea of mud. When road crews paved U.S. 395 in the '30s, they made the automobile trip up from the Southland vastly more inviting. Automobiles had not only caught on as a way to get around in Southern California, but they quickly spawned a culture of their own. Motels were a 1920s Southern California invention, and drive-in restaurants and travel trailers multiplied throughout the state in the 1930s. By the middle of the decade, California had more cars per capita than any other state in the country. Along

with the increase of autos came an explosion of highway tourism, much of it outdoors-loving Californians driving to their own state's beaches, forests, rivers and mountains. Southlanders came in droves to the High Sierra in summer and early fall to hike, fish for trout, or hunt for mule deer, but few ever thought of venturing there for winter recreation.

For the most part, the only people engaging in winter sports in the Eastern Sierra in the early '30s were locals. Ruddy-cheeked residents of the small towns along Highway 395 between Lone Pine and Bridgeport started driving into the nearby mountains for impromptu winter sports parties. Those get-togethers usually included skiing for those few who had skis, while the rest turned to ice skating, tobogganing or the one sport accessible to everyone, sliding down snowy hillsides on ash-can covers. By the winter of 1936, hundreds of people were gathering to skate on the glassy surfaces of June Lake and other frozen lakes. Meanwhile, at Crestview north of Mammoth and at other spots near the highway, dozens of skiers were testing the hillsides.

All of this winter activity convinced the U.S. Forest Service to build a pond for ice skating at Whitney Portal at the bottom of the Mount Whitney trail, and to keep the 10-mile road to it cleared for skaters and skiers. Jane Fisher, who went on to serve several terms as mayor of Bishop, was a teenager in the mid-1930s and remembers skating at the new Whitney Portal pond and drinking hot chocolate next to a big bonfire. "The idea was to get off in the shadows on the other side of the fire so we could sneak in a little necking. That was the main pastime of Owens Valley kids, to sneak away from the adults and neck a little bit," she says.

Soon, locals had identified enough good skiing areas in the Sierra close to Highway 395 to keep them busy on weekends. They skied at Gray's Meadow above Independence, McGee Mountain at Long Valley, Mammoth Mountain, Crestview and June Mountain. Skiers also shuttled up the highway in cars to the top of Conway Summit near Lee Vining, schussed down an

Three pioneers of Eastern Sierra skiing (left to right):
Dave McCoy, Tex Cushion and Max Zischank.

adjacent canyon to a ranch near the lake shore, then caught a ride in another auto back up again.

Most local skiers were self-taught, and they exhibited more pluck than style or technique. Bishop doctor C.L. Scott, who was among the most prominent of the early Eastern Sierra skiers, recalled decades later, "Locals used to find a little hill, put on their high boots, pack the skis over their shoulders, climb up, then point them down. At the bottom of the hill the boots would [slip out] of the toe straps and [the skiers] would fall, only to [get] up and do it again."

The late summer of 1935 was when athletic 20-year-old Dave McCoy arrived in Independence. Already in love with skiing, McCoy and two friends built the first rope tows ever erected in the Eastern Sierra. The original one was a fixed tow powered by a Model A truck

that they parked in Gray's Meadow above the Owens Valley town. They also built a portable tow that they carted up to Crestview—or anyplace else with deep powder. "Probably about 40 or 50 people out of Independence would come up to Gray's Meadow to ski. It was a social. It wasn't what you would call a real adventurous sort of thing. It was more like, 'Hey, let's all go on a picnic,'" McCoy recalls.

Meanwhile, fascination with snow and ice sports was growing in Los Angeles. Around 8,000 Angelenos had turned out at Lake Arrowhead for one of the annual winter sports carnivals that L.A. civic groups began hosting in the late 1920s, featuring ski jumping exhibitions, ice hockey, ski races and tobogganing. By the early 1930s, the Lake Arrowhead Ski Hill was one of several ski areas newly established in the San Gabriel and San Bernardino mountains, although they all suffered from spotty snowfall. Angelenos were thrilled when their city was chosen to host the 1932 Summer Olympics, and they were even more excited when the state Olympic committee tried to make Los Angeles the site of the Winter Games that year as well. Those hopes turned out to be unrealistic, however. The International Olympic Committee, convinced that Southern California lacked the snow or skiing infrastructure to host the Winter Games, rejected the bid, as well as others from Yosemite and Lake Tahoe, awarding the Games to Lake Placid, New York, instead.

Even so, when skiing caught the imagination of the United States sporting public in the wake of the 1932 Winter Games, California became one of the most ski-crazy states. Most often, Southern Californians were introduced to the sport through local ski clubs like the Lake Arrowhead club, which had been among the first ones formed in the 1920s. Arrowhead was followed by several more, including the Edelweiss and Big Pines ski clubs and the Ski Mountaineers of California (later the Ski Mountaineers of the Sierra Club). The groups put together ski trips for their members

and organized ski races, often using the events as vehicles for promoting the sport. By the end of the 1930s, ski clubs had sprouted all over the Southland. Skiers in Long Beach, Pomona, Redlands, San Gabriel, Santa Ana, Glendale and San Diego all formed their own clubs, as did most Southern California colleges and universities.

The Ski Mountaineers, established by a UCLA zoology professor named Walter Mosauer, particularly wanted to advance skiing by teaching it to novices. While the original members of the club were excellent skiers, club-sponsored races were open to all entrants and usually included a good sprinkling of beginners. Wolfgang Lert,

McGee Mountain's easy accessibility and wide-open, perfectly pitched slopes made it the most popular skiing spot in the 1930s.

an early Ski Mountaineer and member of the UCLA ski team, recalls the club's first downhill race, held on Mount San Antonio. With no lift to the top, the racers had to make a long, muscle-knotting climb to the starting line. After they reached it and caught their breaths, they strapped on their skis and launched themselves back down the course. Lert started in the middle of the pack, but after racing partway down, he caught his ski pole on a tree branch.

"It spun me around a few times and down the hill," says Lert. "I wasn't going to leave my pole up there, because it was a two- or three-hour climb, so I went back up to the tree, got my pole and continued on. The race went around the edge of the mountain, and there I saw everybody who had started before me lying on the snow and waving their legs in the air."

Lert carved a few wide turns around the prostrate racers and tucked to the finish line, winning easily.

Mosauer and Lert were accomplished ski mountaineers who made a variety of ambitious ski treks in the Eastern Sierra, including one above Bishop Creek Canyon with legendary mountain climber Norman Clyde. Mosauer also led a group that climbed from Conway Summit up 12,374-foot Dunderberg Peak, and another arduous trek up nearby Mount Warren, which turned out to be more perilous than Lert expected.

"We climbed it from the back and skied down the front," he remembers. "It turned out to be the most horrifying breakable crust all the way down. We survived, but we had to make lots of gorilla turns."

Mosauer and Lert were also among the early skiers on Mammoth Mountain, trekking over the mountain years before anyone ever attempted to put a tow there. Mosauer, one of California's early laureates of skiing, also founded the UCLA ski team and wrote a series of magazine articles about the sport and a book, *On Skis Over the Mountains*. Sadly, he perished after eating poisonous plants while on a research expedition to Mexico at the age of 32.

Despite the growing interest in winter sports among Southern Californians, few Eastern Sierra locals immediately saw the commercial possibilities they offered. One exception was a sharp, civic-minded Bishop drugstore owner and avid skier named George

The moon sets as the sun rises on the Sierra Crest. Scenes like this have inspired generations of Eastern Sierra enthusiasts.

In the 1920s and 1930s, some owners of Mammoth Lakes cabins built their own rope tows. Above, left: Tex Cushion positioned one behind his Winter Patrol Station (in background). Above, right: His next-door neighbor, Dr. H.F. Rey, had a perfect view of Mammoth Mountain from the top of his tow.

Deibert. In 1936, Deibert pointed out to a reporter that local businessmen were always primed to advance the Eastern Sierra's summertime fishing and camping tourism. "But when winter comes we go into hibernation. We are passing up a great opportunity," he insisted.

Deibert, who later became known as "Mr. Bishop" for his tireless promotion of the area, became the main catalyst for starting the first winter sports club on the Sierra's east slope. The Eastern Sierra Ski Club was born in Bishop on January 1, 1937, with Deibert as its first president. Club members immediately concentrated on finding road crews to keep the routes to the most popular mountain areas clear of snow. At first the club was preoccupied with ice skating, but the focus soon shifted to skiing, with the idea of drawing in the "vast reservoir of winter receptionists" waiting on the southern end of Highway 395, as the local newspaper, the *Inyo Independent*, put it.

It didn't take long for word to reach Southern California about the hip-deep snow and the new emphasis on winter sports in the Eastern Sierra, and some of the more adventuresome Southern California skiers began driving up from L.A. to try it out. Among

Bishop drug store owner George Deibert was among the first locals to recognize the economic potential of winter sports for the Eastern Sierra.

them was Jack Northrop, the famed aeronautical engineer who went on to design many successful aircraft for the American military, including the "flying wing." John Rey, the son of the Swiss doctor who had taught Tex Cushion how to ski, was still a boy when he watched Northrop jack up his car on Cushion's property in Old Mammoth and attach a homemade device to his rear wheel to power a primitive rope tow.

"Northrop got tired of walking up the hill," recalls Rey, "and he said, 'I've had enough of this.' He had a rope that went from the automobile to a pulley on a tree—it wasn't even 100 yards long." One day, as young Rey looked on, Northrop, Cushion and Dave McCoy took turns on the makeshift tow. "One of them would sit in the driver's seat and put it in low gear," Rey remembers. "They'd play games, like the guy in the driver's seat would goose it and the other guy on skis would fall on his nose." It was the first ski tow ever installed at Mammoth.

Northrop, who had by then already started his own aviation company, toyed with the idea of designing a more permanent tow on Mammoth Mountain and enlisted Cushion in the project, but they quickly abandoned the idea because of the mountain's remoteness.

An "Irish devil," his friend Andrea Mead Lawrence liked to call him, Hill would often amuse his cohorts with mischievous pranks.

International Ski Federation (FIS).

Lawrence, who would become a longtime Mammoth Lakes resident and elected official, had first met Hill when she was a 15-year-old skier on the 1948 U.S. Olympic team and Hill was the team's manager. The railroad heir and his elegant wife, Blanche, chaperoned the young ski team on the boat voyage to the Winter Games at St. Moritz, Switzerland.

making sure the transportation was set up for us, the hotels were all lined up, doing all the things it takes to move a team around," Lawrence remembers. "He was independently wealthy, but he did it because he loved skiing, he loved these young people. That was just his persona." Hill greatly encouraged Lawrence in her racing career, and she honored him in return. When she gave birth to her first son in 1953, she named him Cortlandt after

Above, left: Corty Hill's wife Blanche (left) hands Ethel Severson (later Van Degrift) the trophy for winning the first women's slalom ever organized in the Eastern Sierra. Above, right: Former Tamarack Lodge caretaker Nan Zischank, who opened Nan and Max's Long Valley Resort with her husband, became one of the top female ski racers in the Eastern Sierra.

their new Tyrol Ski School, and Hess and his two brothers learned how to ski from those masters. Unfortunately, during the venture's first winter, the area received its lightest snowfall in decades, and while Lee Vining's handful of residents became very well schooled in proper skiing technique, the enterprise soon closed.

Hess took part in one of the most perilous ski races ever held in the Eastern Sierra. The Flying Skis race, organized by the Mono Ski Club, started above 11,000 feet on the near-vertical slopes of Carson Peak close to June Lake. It plunged down the extreme Devil's Chute and dropped for five miles and 4,000 vertical feet to the finish line. The race began at 10:30 in the morning, so racers had to rise before dawn to ascend to the

Zischank received the George Deibert Perpetual Trophy for winning an Inyo-Mono Women's Championship early in the 1940s.

starting line. Hess recalls, "It took us four and a half, five hours to climb up to the top, because it was so steep. Right at the last you'd have to kick steps going up. Then it took about four minutes to come down." Nan Zischank and Clarita Heath were the only two women to ever compete in the race. Zischank recalled, "You stood there and they said, 'Five, four, three, two, one, go!' and you looked down and didn't see anything under your skis."

Pasadena skier Chris Schwarzenbach won the race that first year, while Hess came in fourth. "We didn't have any ski patrol. If you got hurt there, it was quite a while before anyone would get to you," Hess says.

Zischank, recalling her finish in the second annual race, said, "I was the last racer and Frank Springer from Los Angeles was just ahead of me. He broke through the snow just before the finish gate and caught his ski on a sagebrush, and he got eight spiral breaks in his leg. He just lay there yelling…he was so hurt. Everybody gathered around him, and here I came. The further down I got, the less I could find a spot to get through. Tex Cushion always said, 'Don't run into anything, sideswipe it,' so I did and I

Opposite: Carson Peak near June Lake was the site of the electrifying, short-lived Flying Skis races in the early 1940s.

You can't keep a good man down: A shirtless Dave McCoy entertained himself with ski stunts.

took people, Springer, the whole bit with me, bodies clanging together, and the two of us went through the finish gate together." Zischank, Springer and several other entrants landed in the hospital. That was the last time the race was ever held.

By the end of the 1930s, the popularity of skiing was booming in Los Angeles. In 1939, the *Los Angeles Times* became the first major metropolitan newspaper in the country to hire a regular winter-sports writer—Ethel Severson, the former Paramount secretary. Severson, who was soon to marry the Los Angeles ski shop owner and become Ethel Van Degrift, not only promoted skiing in her writings and encouraged Angelenos to try the sport, but had also developed a special affection for the Eastern Sierra and its magnificent panoramas and endless deep-powder slopes. In her biweekly articles, she began to report regularly on skiing developments at McGee Mountain and other popular Eastern Sierra skiing spots, and included snow and weather dispatches about the area with her roundup of conditions in the Southern California mountains.

That was when Mammoth Mountain's fame began to grow.

Ethel Van Degrift loved the Eastern Sierra ski slopes and spread the word about them in her *Los Angeles Times* column "Ski Slants."

One of the first magazine articles ever written about the huge ski mountain appeared in the March 1939 issue of a magazine called *Ski Heil* (a common ski greeting that fell out of use after World War II, for obvious reasons). It raved, "Have you not been searching for the ultimate perfect slopes—the veritable skiers' Utopia, the perfection of which could not be surpassed—the place where you could double the length of your ski season? Now you need look no farther, for Mammoth Mountain with its broad white-blanketed buttresses and remarkably beautiful scenery is the answer to your prayers. Here good spring skiing may be enjoyed far into July, long after snow has disappeared on other ski slopes."

Not long after that article appeared, the California Ski Association decided to hold its state championships there. The visiting dignitaries were thoroughly impressed with Mammoth Mountain, despite snow flurries on Saturday that grew into a near-blizzard that threatened the competition on Sunday. According to the *Bridgeport Chronicle-Union*, gale winds blew some skiers clear across the icy course and enveloped others in a swirling, frozen fog,

Tom's Place became one of the aprés-ski hangouts for people skiing McGee Mountain and other Long Valley locations.

forcing the cross-country event to be moved to nearby Crestview. As Van Degrift described it, "Sharp ice particles slashed at one's face. Icicles formed on eyelashes and beards. We stubbornest spectators huddled around a smoky fire." Even so, Joel Hildebrand, a University of California chemistry professor and skiing authority who set the race course, called the Eastern Sierra the finest skiing terrain he had seen in the state. A ski writer from the *San Francisco Examiner* added that it was the first time the state championship downhill race had been run "down a real mountain."

Word about the Eastern Sierra's excellent skiing continued to spread, and no one did more to publicize the region than Ethel Van Degrift, who soon became the associate editor of a new national magazine, *Ski Illustrated*, in addition to continuing to write her *Los Angeles Times* column. In an article for her magazine, she trilled,

THE WATER WARS

In 1904, Fred Eaton and William Mulholland came to the Eastern Sierra from Los Angeles on a mission that ultimately transformed the destiny of both places. The two men were officials of the Los Angeles City Water Company, and their plan was to surreptitiously buy up the irrigated farmland of the Owens Valley, using front agents pretending to be farmers or ranchers. Once they secured the land and its attendant water rights, they began building an aqueduct to channel the full flow of the Owens River to Los Angeles. The water grab enabled the city to grow into a metropolis, and ruined the economy of the Owens Valley.

The opening of the Los Angeles Aqueduct in 1913 marked the beginning of decades of hard times for Owens Valley residents.

As author Marc Reisner wrote in *Cadillac Desert*, "Los Angeles employed chicanery, subterfuge, spies, bribery, a campaign of divide-and-conquer, and a strategy of lies to get the water it needed. In the end, it milked the valley bone-dry, impoverishing it, while the water made a number of prominent Los Angeleans very, very rich." Residents of the ill-starred valley tried to fight back in the 1920s, sometimes dynamiting the hated aqueduct in scenes that could have come straight out of one of the Hollywood westerns often filmed nearby. Once, cowboy actor Tom Mix, who was shooting a movie in the area, stopped by to entertain the valley's water rebels.

The powerful city prevailed in the end. The diversion of the Owens River completely dried up a saline lake near Lone Pine, turning it into a 100-square-mile, wind-blown salt pan. Later, after the city built a second aqueduct and began pumping Owens Valley groundwater into it, the once promising orchard and farmland was slowly transformed into a dusty, desiccated strip. The only industry left to its people was catering to fishermen and other tourists who visited the Eastern Sierra on vacations.

Mammoth Lakes fared much better. Virtually all of the land surrounding the town has long been federally owned and not available for purchase. However, in the 1930s, the city of Los Angeles did buy a ranch of Eaton's down the highway in Long Valley and started constructing a controversial dam for a reservoir to hold the city's water. Los Angeles then acquired more land in the Mono Lake Basin to get control of the freshwater creeks that fed that salt lake, and diverted those waters. The water agency completed its reservoir at Long Valley beneath

McGee Mountain in 1941 and named it Crowley Lake after Father John J. Crowley, who had tried to calm the bitterness between the city and the residents of the Eastern Sierra. A settlement between the city and the residents of Owens Valley was finally reached in the 1990s, but wrangling over water continues to this day between Los Angeles and the people of the valley and, to a lesser degree, of Mono County. ❂

Man-made Crowley Lake is both a reservoir for Los Angeles and a popular Eastern Sierra angling spot.

"All along Highway 395 north of Bishop is ski country. There is a hundred-mile stretch of it that has been likened to the Tyrolean Alps. You can get out of your car and ski anywhere. Never will I forget the first time I saw this part of the Sierra in winter. For two hundred and fifty miles we drove through the most beautiful snow country I had ever seen, endless vistas of mountain snow scenes, each vista more breathlessly beautiful than the last. It didn't seem possible there was so much snow in the world." Adorning that piece, which briefly highlighted the notable virtues of Mammoth Mountain, was a photo of a distinguished-looking Corty Hill and another of a shirtless Dave McCoy on skis.

Around the same time, a newly formed trade organization called the Inyo-Mono Association hired a writer named Bob Brown to be its executive secretary and chief publicist. He began sending out weekly "Snow Bulletins" to 200 media and commercial outlets detailing snow depths, weather conditions and storm forecasts. Brown also helped spread the word by placing photo displays about Eastern Sierra skiing in the windows of Bullocks, May Company and Broadway department stores in Los Angeles and Hollywood, as well as in several Southland sporting goods stores.

In 1940 a snow drought in most of the southern half of California coincided with heavy snowfall in the Sierra, which, together with the region's growing notoriety as a skiing center, brought record numbers of skiers to the area. During the 1939–40 Christmas and New Year's Day holidays, 400 out-of-town skiers, the most ever to descend on the region, joined several hundred local skiers on McGee Mountain, Crestview and Mammoth Mountain, where several portable lifts were operating. An ambitious reporter counted 130 cars, an unprecedented throng, parked at the snow line on Minaret Summit Road. Local lodges at Mammoth, McGee, Crestview and June Lake were packed, with the overflow crowds staying at hotels in Bishop. The record was eclipsed a few weeks later when around 1,000 people, more than half of them from Southern California, hit the area's slopes. The milestones marked the first skiing boom in the Eastern Sierra, and a sign of things to come. ✪

Excellent snow in Long Valley in the 1930s fueled a skiing boom.

Previous page: Winter sunsets like this one over Alkali Lake make
the drive north to Mammoth a visual banquet. Above: Despite
Mammoth Mountain's remoteness in the '30s and '40s, Dave McCoy
remained convinced it was the best site for a ski area because of its
deep, reliable snowpack.

c h a p t e r   3

Young Dave McCoy

One day in the winter of 2002, as Dave McCoy sat in his corner office overlooking Mammoth's Broadway trail, he turned to look out at the waves of skiers cascading down the hill. At 87, after more than 60 years of running lifts on this mountain, who would have blamed him if he were gazing outside to reminisce? Maybe about the time he had first skied Mammoth's bowls when he was just a few years out of high school. Or the time he stayed up all night putting the finishing touches on the mountain's first chairlift. Or the year it snowed so heavily that the chairlifts were buried and drifts engulfed the three-story main lodge.

As he looked out his office window that sun-drenched morning, it wasn't the past he was thinking about, but the future. "I see it today for tomorrow," he said. "How can I make it better? How can I use that pile of snow there, spread it out to eliminate that sidehill? I'm always finding something to do."

It has always been one of McCoy's principal characteristics that he never stops thinking about making things work better—new lifts, improved grooming, a new configuration of trails. In the 1960s

he came up with a novel way to build chairlifts, using adjustable lift terminals that could be set for different snow levels, which became the industry standard. He was a pioneer of hill grooming, from the early days when he dragged sets of 50-gallon drums behind prototype snow vehicles, to conceptualizing the winch cats now used to groom ultrasteep slopes. In the 1950s and '60s, he also became one of the best ski race coaches in the country; some say *the* best. His racers won so many competitions that they focused interna-

The rising sun warms 13,157-foot Mount Ritter and 12,945-foot Banner Peak in the Mammoth backcountry.

tional attention on Mammoth. Many of his young skiers went on to compete in the Olympics.

McCoy started Mammoth Mountain in 1953, relying on his own labor and the volunteered help of a few friends in lieu of capital. Until 1996, when Vancouver-based Intrawest Corporation bought a significant stake in the operation, McCoy and his family still owned the ski area outright. (McCoy retained a controlling interest after the sale.) His original weekend hobby, running free rope tows for his skiing friends, turned into one of the biggest and best-run ski operations in the country, grossing nearly $100 million a year. McCoy and everyone who knows him say that it was never money he was after, and that when he started he had no thought of someday building a ski area with 27 lifts and 150 trails. He was just passionate about skiing and loved being outside in the snow and the clean Sierra Nevada air. As it happened, his other passion was for machinery. McCoy has always been endlessly fascinated with gears, wheels and engines. Those two seemingly incongruous interests blended together seamlessly and produced Mammoth Mountain.

As a young man, McCoy worked as a laborer and a soda jerk; he picked grapes and sold firewood. He was always a positive thinker and a tireless worker, a man with simple tastes and a sensible way of looking at things, down-to-earth, determined, and patient. And lucky. After all, what could be luckier than starting a ski resort just a few years before the popularity of the sport exploded in the wake of the 1960 Winter Olympics at Squaw Valley?

Or maybe McCoy made his own luck. By the 1960s he had turned down several opportunities to leave Mammoth for endeavors that most would have considered more promising, and fended off a host of big money offers over the years to sell his budding ski operation. He was at Mammoth because that was where he wanted to be.

In his younger days, McCoy was muscular and tough. Even at the age of 87, he is still phenomenally fit, taking 26-mile mountain-bike rides around Mammoth Lakes and the Owens Valley, climbing steep hills and bush-whacking through scrub and forest that would exhaust riders 50 years younger. And frequently trying out the motocross bike his employees had presented him as a birthday gift. He had always been health conscious, a lifelong teeto-taler who never smoked and who began popping multivitamins, downing food supplements and consulting with nutritionists years before it became fashionable.

McCoy was strikingly handsome as a young man, with wavy blonde hair, a square jaw and a halogen grin. His friend Cortlandt Hill thought he had the looks to succeed in Hollywood and even attempted to persuade him to try a career as an actor, but the young man knew he had little acting ability and even less interest in it. Besides, he had other plans.

McCoy was born in 1915 in El Segundo, California, just south of Los Angeles, the son of a stern father from whom he inherited a strong work ethic, a love for sports and an interest in mechanical things. "It was common in those days to [grease and oil your own cars], to tear a motor down on a weekend so it would run the next week. [My father] saw to it that I helped him."

His father was a paving contractor, an occupation that forced the family to relocate frequently to road construction sites throughout Southern California and up and down the Central Valley. McCoy spent a rootless, restless adolescence, sometimes attending as many as a dozen different schools in a single year. When he was 13, he and his mother traveled for a vacation to the town of Independence in the Eastern Sierra, where a family friend took him hiking in the high mountains and fishing in backcountry lakes surrounded by vast pine forests. The rugged beauty of the Sierra Nevada rising above the arid Owens Valley floor left an indelible impression on him.

A few years later, his childhood was rocked when his mother and father separated. They sent him to live with his paternal grandparents, whom he had never met before, in the little town of Wilkeson, Washington, in the shadow of Mount Rainier. It wasn't until then that he found out, to his surprise, that his family name wasn't McCoy, and he wasn't Irish. When his father had left home as a young man, he had changed his name from Cox to McCoy on an impulse.

His grandparents treated him well, but the 15-year-old couldn't get used to Washington's damp weather. "I was there for 90 days, and I couldn't stand it—rain, rain, rain, rain. I was a sunshine boy,

Above: Dave McCoy's contractor father traveled throughout central and southern California building roads, including the coastal Highway 101. Below: Young Dave McCoy returned to Washington to visit his grandfather (right) in the mid 1930s.

a California boy. So I hitchhiked back to California, worked in a grocery store, cut grapes, tended pigs for room and board."

He became increasingly independent, hitchhiking back and forth between Washington and California several times. He jumped freight trains and a few times stayed in the hobo jungles that had sprung up after the Depression.

"Sometimes I was living with the bums at the edge of a creek, sitting by the campfires or by the canned heat where the guys would be cooking," McCoy recalls "I was the little kid there, and people tried to take care of me."

McCoy says those experiences toughened him up and built character and self-reliance. He distinguished himself as a high school athlete in Washington, lettering in track, basketball and football, and was named an all-state receiver and defensive back. He wasn't tall, but he was powerfully built, agile, well-coordinated and exceptionally swift. A childhood friend swore that he once watched McCoy chase down and catch a jackrabbit on foot. Most importantly, he was dependable.

"I was a short-distance runner, long-distance runner, hurdler, broad jumper—whatever they wanted to put me in. I was never really the best at those sports, except in football, but I was always right there and I could do whatever they needed," McCoy says. He also developed his growing interest in the outdoors in Washington, often accompanying his grandfather and his friends on hiking and fly-fishing trips.

One year while he was still in high school, young McCoy watched spellbound as Austrian ski instructor Otto Lang, who later headed Sun Valley's ski school, put on a ski-jumping exhibition at Washington's Snoqualmie Pass. The following winter the teenager built himself a pair of skis out of ash in his school's wood shop and

Above: While still in high school in Washington, McCoy (center) learned to ski with his buddies Joe Logan (left) and Americo Bostenero (right).
Below: When he first moved to the Owens Valley town of Independence, McCoy worked as a soda jerk at Jim's Restaurant.

used steam from a boiler at the mine where his grandfather worked to bend the tips. He attached the homemade skis to his logging boots with pieces of inner tube and tried them out on the slopes where Crystal Mountain resort is located today, near 14,410-foot-high Mount Rainier. The youngster was immediately hooked. He loved the speed and freedom of gliding down snowy hillsides and vaulting off jumps. Later, he tested his skis at White Pass south of Wilkeson, and went ski trekking on Rainier.

After McCoy finished high school, he knew where he wanted to go: back to Independence, California, in the Eastern Sierra. Hitchhiking south, he caught a ride with a deliveryman who had several stops in Mammoth Lakes before he could continue on to the Owens Valley. The driver dropped McCoy off near Penney's Bakery on the outskirts of town, where the teenager waited while the man finished his deliveries, shading his eyes and gazing up at gargantuan Mammoth Mountain, still partly mantled with snow in the middle of summer. McCoy felt an immediate, powerful connection with the place, and says that he somehow already knew that he was going to spend his life there.

After he arrived in Independence, he went to work as a soda jerk at a restaurant in town. From behind the counter, the shy but personable young man soon met hydrographers from the Los Angeles Department of Water and Power, whose regional headquarters were located in the town. Their job mainly involved skiing through the Sierra backcountry measuring the snowpack to predict the following year's water supply for the city, which sounded to young McCoy like a dream job.

During the winter of 1935, he carved a new pair of skis out of ash and hauled them up to Gray's Meadow in the Sierra above Independence. He and his new buddies from the water department

built the Sierra's first rope tow out of an old truck frame and engine mainly so that they could ski themselves, but other locals soon began drifting up to try the new sport.

"I was the one who was excited about it," McCoy recalls. "I guess I was going to go skiing whether anyone else went or not, and others decided they wanted to try it too."

While the popularity of skiing was beginning to germinate in the Eastern Sierra, his hydrographer friends invited the 21-year-old McCoy to accompany them on their regular three-day survey on Mammoth Mountain the following spring, checking the snow depths in what was then lonely backcountry. They started the ski tour at Lake Mary on the mountain's southeast side and climbed from there up to Mammoth Pass, then cut across to where the ski area's Canyon Lodge sits today before finishing the route by ascending to Minaret Summit. It was the first time McCoy ever skied on the big mountain, and he was exhilarated, diving down its

McCoy spent almost two decades ski mountaineering through the Sierra backcountry checking the snowpack for the Los Angeles Department of Water and Power.

SIERRA BIGHORN REDUX

ighorn sheep have roamed the rocky high reaches of the Sierra for millennia, but over the past 20 years they nearly disappeared from the range. Their troubles actually started back when settlers started streaming into the area in the 1800s and overhunted the animals. A menu that survives from one 19th-century Bodie restaurant lists bighorn sheep as an entrée. Hunting the sheep has long been outlawed, but Bishop wildlife researcher John Wehausen, the foremost authority on Sierra bighorn sheep who works at the town's University of California White Mountain Research Station, says that other modern threats nearly led to their extinction. Despite their image as an indestructible creature because of the ferocious horn-bashing melees of the rams, bighorns are highly vulnerable to diseases transmitted by domestic sheep grazing near them, and are sometimes easy prey for mountain lions. Biologists say the combination was the cause of their recent decline.

Sierra bighorns have gone through their ups and downs since the late 1970s. After the California Department of Fish and Game found that the sheep's numbers had nose-dived, the agency began capturing bighorns and moving them by helicopter in the 1980s to reestablish herds in parts of their native range where they had disappeared. Some were relocated to the mountains above Lee Vining just outside of Yosemite National Park. In the first few years of the program, the bighorns' numbers rose from around 250 to more than 300, but then the population crashed again, reaching a low of around 100 animals by 1996. Finally, after Wehausen and another researcher were able to document that Sierra bighorns were a separate subspecies, the animals were declared an endangered species in 1999. Now, separated from domestic sheep and with mountain lion numbers down, the bighorns are on the rise again.

Bighorns don't roam the mountains near Mammoth today, but even most locals would probably be surprised to learn that the animals used to wander over Mammoth Mountain's rocks in the summertime, and not that long ago. One bighorn herd used to dwell in the Convict Creek drainage on Bloody and Laurel mountains south of Mammoth.

Biologists reestablished a Sierra bighorn herd in Lee Vining Canyon just outside of Yosemite National Park.

"They actually made it into the 1950s as a native herd," Wehausen says. "I suspect those sheep crossed over Mammoth Mountain, because there's evidence that they were using San Joaquin Ridge," he says of the ridgetop about a mile northeast of the Mammoth Mountain Main Lodge. A deer hunter illegally shot a ram on the ridge in 1954. Mammoth Mountain was probably a key corridor for the animals, Wehausen notes, adding that the herd most likely perished because of contact with the domestic sheep that used to graze all around the area in summer.

Bighorns are highly vulnerable to diseases transmitted by domestic sheep grazing near them.

McCoy powers through the downhill at the first Eastern Sierra ski race, organized on McGee Mountain in 1937.

steep canyons and across its wide bowls and noting how much deeper its snow was compared with that of the surrounding countryside. After meeting Tex Cushion at his cabin, McCoy was back on Mammoth Mountain a few weeks later, ski trekking with Tex and some of his friends to the top of the big mountain on Easter Sunday.

Later, McCoy grew much more familiar with Mammoth's unpredictable, monumental snowfall when he accompanied another hydrographer into the town. As soon as they arrived at Cushion's cabin, the snow started falling. It didn't let up for 11 days, and when it finally stopped, more than 20 feet of snow had dumped on the town. They skied to check on the Penneys, who were wintering at their new tavern, but were forced to climb in through a second story window. Finding them unscathed, Tex asked Dave to ski to the cabin occupied by a couple named Phillips, who were caretakers at a

Above, left: McCoy (far right) won a slalom at the first Eastern Sierra race, organized by Corty Hill (third from right) and his wife Blanche, standing at his side. Above, right: McCoy, face well-protected from the sun, receives a racing medal from Eastern Sierra Ski Club officer George Deibert.

Mammoth summer retreat known as Valentine Camp.

"He told me about how far it was and how to get to it, but when I got there I couldn't see a cabin or anything, anywhere," McCoy recalls. "I stood around and pondered what to do. Pretty soon I saw a little opening in the snow with a little bit of smoke coming out of it, and heard a strange noise."

The cabin had been completely buried, and the sound was the Phillipses trying to tunnel their way out by shoveling the snow from outside their front door into the cabin. McCoy poked his skis down through the snow to let them know he was there, and then stayed to help them dig out.

McCoy often traveled to ski races around California in the late 1930s and early 1940s.

Once Cortlandt Hill and Jack Northrop built their rope tow at McGee Mountain, McCoy started making the 70-mile trip from Independence to ski there whenever he could. McCoy and Hill quickly became friends, their mutual interest in skiing bridging the wide gulf in their backgrounds. Hill was driving his Cord up from Santa Monica nearly every weekend with a few skiing buddies, and he began stopping at Independence to give McCoy a lift to McGee Mountain, or to Crestview when the snow was better there.

"We would read out of the Northland catalogue, a little ski instruction booklet they put out with their skis that told you how to snowplow and that sort of thing," McCoy says. "Corty had some friends from Austria—Hannes Schneider and his group, Luggi Foegger—all those early champion skiers. We used to critique each other and learn from a day's outing."

McCoy later met Sepp Benedikter, the Austrian ski instructor that Hill had brought to the Eastern Sierra to improve his own skiing, and the two practiced their own early version of snowboarding. "Sepp was just one of us kids. We played 'extreme' at everything. We would take a six-foot toboggan up the cable lift, and then we'd stand up and ride it down the way they rode surfboards, just for fun. We'd hold onto the nose and tweak it and lean just like the kids on snowboards today."

McCoy's skiing kept improving. He had developed a graceful, fluid style, and was jackrabbit quick. When the Eastern Sierra Ski Club began holding local championship races in the late 1930s, he emerged as the top local competitor. He won the overall title several times and one year swept every race, taking the slalom, downhill and cross-country events. He soon began traveling to races around California and is credited with capturing several slalom championships in the late '30s.

In 1937, his skiing prowess finally landed him the job he wanted—doing snow surveys for the Los Angeles Department of Water and Power—although he was originally hired as a laborer.

Above: McCoy (foreground) and other Eastern Sierra Ski Club members caught rides up McGee Mountain on Corty Hill's rope tow. In the background is a stretch of Long Valley now covered by Crowley Lake. Right: McCoy often roared into Long Valley on his Harley, with skis attached.

He used some of his first paychecks to buy a second-hand Harley-Davidson, and he became a striking, familiar figure on the streets of Independence and Bishop. McCoy would come roaring by with his skis strapped to the side of the motorcycle in winter, often wearing no shirt and with a red bandanna tied around his head. The Harley gave the restless young man a new way to explore the world.

"I'd get on the motorcycle and go to Mexico, to Canada," McCoy recalls. "Or I'd get on it and ride to Reno, then over to Frisco, down to Bakersfield and back here. I guess I was a character as far as other people were concerned. I was free-spirited."

Among those who noticed the handsome, shirtless McCoy racing by on his Harley was Roma Carriere, a pretty young woman from Bishop. She had already made an impression on McCoy a few years earlier when she came into the Independence restaurant during his shift, but he had been too shy to talk to her. They met later through her brother, one of McCoy's skiing buddies, but he was still too bashful to ask her out. Roma, whom Dave would marry a few years later, recalls, "I wanted to get a date with him, but in those days you didn't just phone a guy up and say, 'Come on over.' One day a carnival came to town, and there was this wild girl in town who asked him to go. He really didn't want to go with her, so he [lied and] told her he already had a date. But he knew he would see her there, so he asked me to go with him [so he wouldn't be caught lying]. That was our first date."

Once the ice was broken, the pair started spending time together. "I wasn't a lot like him, I had never hiked in the back-country or skied," Roma comments. "The first time he taught me how to ski, we went up to Crestview—that little flat hill, but to me it looked like Mount Everest. We walked up, and he said, 'Now turn around and point your skis straight down.' I was scared to death, but I did that a couple of times. The third time I fell and rolled into a tree well, and I couldn't get out. I asked him to help me, but he said, 'No, you have to learn how to get out by yourself. What if I wasn't here?' So I struggled for a while, but finally I managed to crawl out. That was my first introduction into how tough he was." Under McCoy's schooling, Roma quickly became an excellent skier and a fine racer who took several first-place trophies at the Inyo-Mono Championships.

McCoy often pitched in to help keep the gas-powered McGee lift running. "He'd arrive there on his motorcycle with his skis lashed to the side of it," Hill recalled years later, "and if anything went wrong with the lift, which happened often, he was always ready to help out. Everybody else might go into the warm-

Above: Barbara James (left), wearing the Eastern Sierra Ski Club logo on her arm, and Roma Carriere, holding rope tow gripper, often skied at McGee. Below: Dave taught Roma how to ski before they were married, and she became a champion ski racer.

Above, left: The Wooden Wings Ski Club was made up largely of Hollywood celebrities. Relaxing après ski in the Wooden Wings clubhouse at Tom's Place in 1939, from right to left: Actor Tyrone Power, French actress Annabella (who married Power shortly after this photo was taken), Corty Hill, and actor Richard Greene. Above, right: Frances Fonda waxes skis outside the Wooden Wings clubhouse with ski instructor Sepp Benedikter.

ing hut for a cup of coffee, but Dave went out in the storm with us and fixed the lift. He had a great mechanical sense, a great touch with machinery, young as he was."

In 1938, after a few good years at McGee, the owner of the fox-breeding farm that sat directly across the road complained to the Forest Service that the skiing clamor was disturbing his animals. Hill graciously moved his tow a few miles down the highway to a hillside in a spot he liked called Little Round Valley near Tom's Place, where a store, cabins and gas pump stood. He refurbished the lodge as headquarters for the Wooden Wings Ski Club, comprised mostly of Hollywood celebrities and Los Angeles socialites who drove up Highway 395 to ski. Once Hill had vacated, the Eastern Sierra Ski Club snagged the lift permit for McGee, and McCoy and other club members built a rope tow and installed it a half mile away from the highway and the foxes.

The following year, the club purchased a temperamental portable lift that frequently broke down. Club members counted on McCoy's magic with machinery to help keep their tows running, just as Hill had. The hours he spent coaxing the tows to life cut acutely into his own skiing time, but McCoy enjoyed working on them

Actor Henry Fonda came skiing in the Eastern Sierra with his wife Frances.

about as much as he did carving turns.

"If it wasn't running, someone had to fix it," he explains. "I just happened to be the one that was mechanical minded and liked doing it. It wasn't work, it was fun."

He built a few small portable lifts for the club, and in the fall of 1940, he lugged a 630-foot rope tow onto the deepening snowpack on the north side of Mammoth Mountain. He and a few others skied there until the snow on the access road piled up too high to clear, then they moved back down the highway to McGee. Around that time, the Eastern Sierra Ski Club began losing interest in running its own rope tows, so in 1941 McCoy decided to strike out on his own. He bought the club's erratic portable, stripped it and used the parts to build a more reliable tow fastened onto a six-foot toboggan. After obtaining a "roving permit" from the Forest Service that allowed him to put the portable tow anywhere, he hauled it to Mammoth Mountain, the first time he had his own ski lift on the broad-backed mountain. He and a few friends installed it on the western end of the north face, where the St. Anton run is today, and skied there for weeks. On some days, he and Roma would make two or three climbs to the mountain summit to ski the Cornice, the now-famous bowl named for the broad rim of snow that used to jut over it.

Dave and Roma were married that year in Yuma, Arizona, but their plans to honeymoon in San Francisco were dashed when they stopped in Hollywood and their car was burglarized. They lost most of their money and belongings, and were forced to head home to Bishop. The couple ended up hiking 10 miles from Tom's Place up to Rock Creek Lake in the Sierra and honeymooning instead at a Los Angeles water department cabin, spending an idyllic week skiing and fishing. Afterward, they moved into a single room with no kitchen in a Bishop rooming house.

McCoy had to supply gasoline to run his tow, but he never charged anyone to use it. Sometimes, he would trade a lift ride for eggs, milk or bread. One week, however, he and Roma ran out of meal money with Dave's water department paycheck still days away.

Roma remembers, "That week he said to me, 'You know, you're going to have to charge those people to ride, because it's another week before I get my paycheck.' I said '*I'm* going to have to charge

Above: Wooden Wings members skied near Tom's Place at Little Round Valley, where Hill relocated his rope tow after he left McGee Mountain. Below: McCoy and other club members built a rope tow for the Eastern Sierra Ski Club on McGee about a half-mile from where Hill vacated.

FLOUR POWER

Every winter weekend, the parking lot of one little bakery along Highway 395 in Bishop is jammed full of skiers' cars. Erick Schat's Bakkery (that's the way they spell it), which looks like an Old World gingerbread house, is a mandatory roadside stop for tens of thousands of Southern Californians driving to or from Mammoth. Inside, customers walk up to the counter carrying armfuls of Sheepherder or Squaw bread, bags of cheese rolls and coffee cakes, bear claws and cinnamon rolls. They'll cart them down to Los Angeles and other Southland cities, and what their family doesn't eat, they'll bestow on their friends.

Schat's became an institution because it has stood in Bishop for a long time, and because it's very good. Its original incarnation opened in Bishop a hundred years ago as a general store started by the Schoch family from Vienna, Austria.

Back then, "there were 445 farms flourishing, the gold mines were here, the railroad was going," comments owner Erick Schat. "Today, I don't see the railroad, I don't see the farms, there sure isn't much gold mining going on, but the bakery's still here."

In the early days, the bakery's customers included scores of Basque sheepherders who relocated from northern Spain to tend their animals in the mountain pastures of the Eastern Sierra. "They ran bands of sheep right through the dirt streets of Bishop," Schat says. "These guys lived on whiskey and beans and bread."

The Basques convinced Schoch to build a stone oven and showed him how to bake large, round flavorful loaves of bread like the ones they used to eat back home in the Pyrenees. Sheepherder bread is today Schat's most famous and widely copied product. Similar-looking versions of the loaves often turn up on the shelves of supermarkets and other bakeries. To make their bread, the Bishop bakery imported special radiant-heat ovens from Germany, and Schat notes that one of his shop's secrets is the natural fermentation process they use.

"Good bread takes time," Schat says. "We still bake it in stone ovens,

Owner Erick Schat with two fragrant loaves from his oven.

Schat's Bakkery has become a Bishop institution.

the way they bake it in the Pyrenees, on the hearth." His son Paul opened a Schat's bakery in Mammoth Lakes several years ago, selling some of the same breads and pastries.

Schat grew up in Holland and came to the United States with his family when he was a boy. He started helping out in the family's bakery in Holland when he was 10, and five years later started working in the Bishop bakery that his family bought in

pounds of flour, 100,000 pounds of cheese and 75,000 pounds of raisins. In 1979 Schat moved up the street from his old location after he built his current bakery, an ornate building with a blue tile roof and a few trim flower gardens in front that is hard to miss from the highway. He says that on their busiest day of the year several thousand people come through the little bakery, even though they don't advertise in Southern California. "Not

them? I can't do that!' He said, 'I can't either. I'm too busy running the tows. See if you can get 50 cents.'"

Roma stood at the bottom of the tow with a cigar box and reluctantly collected 50 cents from each skier. At the end of the day, she looked in the box and proudly counted up $15. She rode up the lift and showed it to her husband, declaring, "We eat tonight!"

Shortly afterward, McCoy aced his civil-service exam and was awarded the coveted Long Valley district hydrographer position, which involved measuring the snowpack between Tom's Place and the Owens River headwaters north of Mammoth. The couple was able to move into a water-department house on a hill overlooking the newly created Crowley Lake, with fine views of both McGee and Mammoth Mountain across the deep-blue water. He worked a few extra jobs, guiding fishermen on the lake and chopping and selling firewood, and on weekends he operated his tow at McGee, Mammoth or wherever else the snow was best. Dave, Roma and a few others were skiing on the north side of Mammoth on December 7, 1941, when he slid down to get their lunch from the car. As he reached for their sandwiches, he flipped on the radio just in time to hear the shocking reports about the Japanese attack on Pearl Harbor. McCoy returned to the hill and relayed the grim news to his friends, then began packing their gear to go home. Once the United States entered the war, Southern Californians restricted to using gasoline coupons weren't able to travel, and the number of out-of-town skiers in the Eastern Sierra dropped off dramatically. After the initial shock passed, however, McCoy resumed running rope tows on weekends and continued for the rest of the winter. During the war's

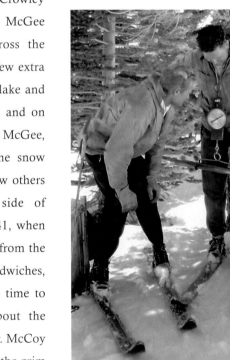

McCoy (at right above and left below) worked with other Los Angeles Department of Water and Power hydrographers measuring the Sierra winter snow pack.

first few months, he considered joining the Navy even though his hydrographer position exempted him from military service, but that decision was soon taken out of his hands.

At season's end in April 1942, McCoy made a spur-of-the-moment decision to drive to Sugar Bowl to compete in the state ski championships. Entrants were supposed to take one prerace run to inspect the course, but on his way there McCoy spotted a hydrographer measuring water in the Truckee River and couldn't resist stopping to talk shop. He arrived at the race late and never took his advance look at the course. Speeding downhill during his first run, McCoy skittered over a snow bridge that gave way under his weight. His left leg slammed into the solid edge of hard-packed snow on the other side of a trough that opened, shattering the bones. McCoy managed to stay upright, skidding downhill on his right leg, but a horde of spectators was standing at the turn directly in front of him. He hollered that he had broken his leg, trying to get them to clear an opening, but with all the commotion of the race they couldn't hear him. McCoy dropped to the snow to avoid hitting the crowd. As he slid and tumbled, the broken bones splintered and severely lacerated the interior of his leg. By the time he stopped rolling, the limb was broken in 28 places, and the leg's interior was hemorrhaging badly.

The view of the Minarets remains just as spectacular today as it was in the 1940s.

The young racer was taken to St. Mary's Hospital in Reno, Nevada. McCoy was shocked by the doctor's diagnosis. "Right away they said they wanted to amputate, but I wouldn't stand for it." McCoy remembers. "I told him, 'Nothing doing.'"

The doctor asked Roma for her consent to take the leg off, but she responded angrily.

"I said 'No way,' Roma recalls. "He didn't give you permission, did he?'"

The doctor then tried McCoy's mother, but she also refused.

"Their goal was to cut that gosh-darned thing off," McCoy recalls. "The doctor said, 'Well, then we'll just let you set there until gangrene sets in.' They took a big sheet and made a sling out of it and put the leg up, and I just laid there for days."

For 21 days, in fact. Finally a visiting doctor from San Francisco asked to look at the young ski racer.

"He said he thought he could fix it, if he could give it a try," McCoy recalls. "I said, 'Okay, let's go to it.'"

The operation took five hours, and the doctor wrapped the bones with wire. It saved the leg and enabled McCoy to leave the hospital and go home, but it didn't heal right. He could hobble around, but the limb wasn't stable. He was forced to switch positions with his hydrographer friend Sam Griggs, taking his desk job in Independence while Griggs took over his Long Valley route. He went to Los Angeles for a second operation the following year, and then for a bone graft the year after that. Finally, after the third operation, the leg began to heal and he was able to walk on it without a brace, although he continued to limp for years afterward and it never really stopped troubling him. He was able to take his hydrography route back, but the accident halted his ski racing career when he was entering his prime and eliminated any possibility of joining the military. He continued working for the water department through World War II, and ran rope tows on weekends for those few people who showed up to ski. ✿

Low clouds enshroud Long Valley and the Eastern Sierra mountains.

Previous page: A single cloud perches characteristically atop Mammoth Mountain (distant right) while the rest of the Sierra stretches beneath blue skies. Above: Moon over Mammoth: The town of Mammoth Lakes gleams at the foot of the big mountain.

chapter 4

Mammoth Dreams

Hans Georg came to the Eastern Sierra from Switzerland in the late 1930s after working at the St. Moritz Ski School and quickly hooked up with the McGee Creek Lodge as a ski instructor. He arrived touting a new skiing technique called the reverse shoulder method that involved weighting the uphill ski and using the hips to propel turns, claiming that it was a faster, easier and safer way to learn the sport than the commonly used Arlberg method.

In addition to becoming the best-known ski instructor in the early days of Eastern Sierra skiing, the young Georg would soon become Dave McCoy's chief rival for the prize of building a ski resort on Mammoth Mountain.

In most ways, Georg could not have been more the opposite of McCoy. Where McCoy was reserved, self-effacing and amiable, Georg was flamboyant, boastful and tactless, and also possessed no real mechanical skill. Even two of the ski instructor's close friends, his ski students and fellow Eastern Sierra Ski Club members Joe and Opal Miller, called Georg his own worst enemy. Opal said, "He had a positive knack for making people dislike him." What Georg and McCoy did have in common was skiing talent and a love for the slopes of the Eastern Sierra.

After ski instruction, Georg's greatest gift was for self-promotion. He set up attention-grabbing exploits that made good copy, such as performing ski exhibitions with six beautiful women doing the same stunts, or skiing on L.A.'s sandy beaches with a cluster of bathing-suited models. Georg made well-publicized ski ascents of Mount Whitney, failing to reach the top the first time but succeeding on a second attempt. He was colorful enough, and he hustled enough, to attract the attention of newspapers all over Southern California and from San Francisco to New York. The media accounts often depicted him as a larger-than-life character. An announcer for Los Angeles radio station KEHE, describing Georg, trumpeted, "This chunky brown package of Swiss skiing dynamite, the last word in grace and style and poise on skis, pirouettes and zooms all over the place. The elite of movieland, society and the sports world come together under his spellbinding leadership and absorb the intricacies of the world of skiing." In his own ski school brochure, Georg hailed himself as an "ingenious instructor and stylist" who was "in the true word a maestro."

Georg may have been self-absorbed, but he meant well. In his Mammoth cabin, he wrote newspaper and magazine articles, columns and several books about skiing, including one entitled *Skiing Simplified*. He always wrote and spoke glowingly about the fine ski slopes of the Eastern Sierra, and in the 1940s became one of the writers who did the most to publicize skiing in the area.

It seems inevitable that with Georg's talent for hype, he would end up in Hollywood. After the war started, he began working as a choreographer for movie ski sequences and wrote one screenplay, a war story. He soon traded cinematic combat tales for real ones, leaving to join the U.S. Army 10th Mountain Division, where he taught skiing to the troops before serving in Italy. At war's end, he returned to the Eastern Sierra and reestablished his ski school, this time setting himself up for business at Mammoth as well as McGee. He bought a rope tow already installed on Mammoth Mountain's east side (near where the Eagle Express chair runs today) from a local fishing guide named Nyle Smith, built a ski hut there and used it as his base of operations.

In the early 1940s, Eastern Sierra skiers were making an unhappy discovery. The deep snow on McGee Mountain that had given them so many pleasurable ski days in the 1930s, turned out to be an aberration. Conditions on McGee Mountain reverted to normal—that is, it didn't snow there much anymore. Cortlandt Hill was forced to abandon his rope tow at Little Round Valley near Tom's Place a few years after he moved it there because the snow rarely even covered the sagebrush. McGee fared only slightly better. Dave McCoy, still hobbled by his leg injury, had built two fixed tows on McGee Mountain that stretched more than a half mile up the hillside, and had also added a warming hut there in the mid 1940s. On days

Above: Hans Georg came to the Eastern Sierra in the 1930s to teach skiing after working at the St. Moritz Ski School in Switzerland. Left and Below: Georg wrote about skiing in newspaper and magazine articles, and he wrote instructional books such as *Skiing Simplified*, which promoted the reverse-shoulder method.

Opposite: Georg built a warming hut for his rope tow operation on Mammoth Mountain's east side, not far from the road to Lake Mary.

Above, left: Dave McCoy purchased Army-surplus Weasels to haul skiers to the otherwise inaccessible north slope of Mammoth Mountain.
Above, right: In later years, the resourceful McCoy, waving, turned snow vehicles into mobile rope tows to transport skiers.

when snow was scarce at McGee, he continued to haul his portable tows to Mammoth's north side.

The problem with operating ski tows on Mammoth Mountain's north-facing slopes was the same as it had always been: They were impossible to reach by car once the snow started piling up. McCoy received little help from the Forest Service clearing the one-lane dirt road to the north side. He could usually keep the road open himself for the first few months of the season, but even then it was so narrow that he had to mark it just to be able to find it under the snow.

Access was Georg's one competitive advantage. His east-side setup was relatively easy to reach, lying at the end of a short dirt track that branched off of the road to the lakes basin, called the Lake Mary Road. In almost every other respect, Georg's operation suffered in comparison to McCoy's. His tows didn't run as smoothly, his area received less snowfall than the north-facing slopes, and the east-side terrain was much less varied and less exciting. Even so, Georg harbored big dreams about developing the east side. He talked about building an aerial tram from his base to the top of Mammoth Mountain, boasting that it would be the

Skiers caught rides up to Gravy Chute on Rope Tow #2. The San Joaquin Ridge looms above them in the background.

longest and highest in the country. He tried to drum up interest in it by billing Mammoth's east side as a possible future venue for a Los Angeles Winter Olympics. For years, Georg begged the Forest Service to allow him to expand his east-side operation, but they never would give him the green light.

Meanwhile, McCoy had his hands full clearing the road, building huts and maintaining and operating his tows. To help him get the job done, he attracted a small regular work crew with a few irresistible qualities: They loved skiing, they were hard workers, and they were willing to work without any pay. Most were Southern Californians fresh out of the service, unsure of what they wanted to do next. The core of the group included three young men: Don Redmon, Toni Milici and Roger Link, joined a few years later by two others, Bob Bumbaugh and Ralph Batchelder. They found working for McCoy to be too much fun to quit. Link recalls, "Dave had the ability to get people to work with him that Hans Georg didn't. I would have worked for Dave the rest of my life for nothing, if I could have figured out some way to survive."

By the end of the 1940s, McCoy devised inventive ways to

solve his transportation problem. He bought a few Studebaker Weasels, a prototype tracked "go-anywhere" vehicle developed for use by the U.S. military during the war. McCoy modified them and slipped 100-foot ropes from the backs to turn them into mobile rope tows. He hauled people for three miles up the hill on their skis from the Lake Mary Road, or sometimes all the way from Mammoth Tavern (formerly Penney's Tavern) on the outskirts of town, putting up to 500 miles a day on the vehicles. Skiers sometimes lost their balance and landed in snow banks, and often arrived happy but chilled to the bone. Later, McCoy bought heavy-duty four-wheel and six-wheel-drive trucks fitted with tire chains that could power over the snow, and used them to shuttle skiers up the mountain.

Eventually, McCoy abandoned McGee Mountain and moved all of his rope tows to Mammoth's north side. He set up one tow driven by a Model A Ford engine where the Broadway Express chair starts now. A second tow deposited skiers beneath the Gravy

Above: The bottom of Rope Tow #1, later replaced by Chair 1, was situated near the current location of the Main Lodge. Below: McCoy's crew putting the finishing touches on the Snake Pit, the little warming hut that got its nickname because its entrance was often buried in snow.

MCCOY TO THE RESCUE

from "The Real McCoy" by Wolfgang Lert

During the early days at Mammoth some of [Dave's] men worked for a pittance, sometimes only for friendship or for the love of skiing. Dave himself put in uncounted hours, days, and nights, without any monetary recompense. On the contrary, between a family that was growing to six healthy, hungry children and a ski area with an apparently insatiable appetite for more and more expensive equipment, Dave was constantly in hock. Yet he never faltered in his dream of building a ski area the way he thought it should be built—nor did he, when he started to be successful, give in to the blandishments of those who offered financial help in order to get in on a "good thing." Today he can look at a solidly established business and say that he took all the risks himself.

And risks there were, beyond the vagaries of snow and weather, for in the beginning Dave did not even have any permanent claim to his hill; he operated only under a year-to-year permit from the Forest Service, though Forest Supervisor

Lacking deep pockets, McCoy built much of Mammoth Mountain with his own two hands. He often worked all day and all night, installing lift towers (above) or doing other heavy construction work (below).

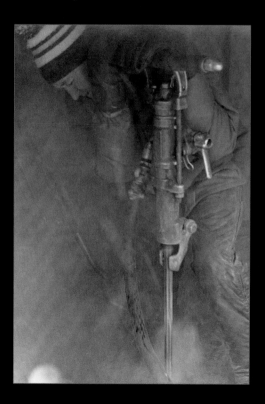

Jimmy Gibson and his local rangers did all in their power to aid the growth of the area. It took years of operation with constantly bigger portable tows before Dave, in 1948, finally graduated to his first permanently installed machinery. Also built around that time, in three hectic days, was the "Snake Pit," Mammoth Mountain's first excuse for a warming hut where, on storm days, a couple of hundred people would crowd into one small room and fight their way within thawing distance of the potbellied stove.

None of the Mammoth pioneers will forget the day when five of Dave's six Weasels broke down, leaving 105 people stranded late in the afternoon in the warming shack which was at that time beneath eighteen feet of snow. Dave finally rigged up a line of some old tow rope and, at 9:00 p.m., managed to tow out all 105 people behind the one remaining Weasel—a laughing, singing, shouting half-mile string of skiers that is likely to stand as a record tow for a long time to come. ✪

—*SKI* Magazine, January 1958

Chute run, and a third climbed from there to the top of a nearby saddle. With Forest Service approval but without a long-term lease, McCoy and his crew began to develop the north side. They cleared trails, cutting down trees with axes and handsaws. They built a little sardine can of a warming hut that became known as the Snake Pit, because snow buried the entrance so deeply that skiers reached it by sliding down a chute. McCoy often worked all night, or went without sleep for an entire weekend, to finish his building projects and still be back at his water-agency job on Monday morning.

He needed his rope-tow income because he had a growing family to support. In 1942, the year he shattered his leg, his first son, Gary, was born. The boy was on skis by the time he was two years old, and when he wasn't, he would walk around with a limp, emulating his father. Between 1945 and 1953, Roma gave birth to five more children: Dennis, Carl, Penny, Kandi and Randy. All six became excellent skiers. Five years after his accident, McCoy's leg finally healed enough that he could go back to ski racing himself. He took the California Championship slalom race in 1948, but by that time he was past his prime, and he turned his attention to teaching racing to young skiers.

Cortlandt Hill, prodded by his disappointing experience at Little Round Valley, dedicated himself to finding the perfect Sierra location for a ski resort. In 1946, he rounded up a group of skiing experts that included his two former ski-instructor friends from St. Anton, Austria—Hannes Schneider and Luggi Foeger—and Forest Service recreation officer Jim Gibson.

Hill took the group flying over the Sierra Nevada looking for the ultimate ski mountain, shooting photographs and marking maps from Southern California to Bend, Oregon. After that, the railroad heir and his friends motored up and down Sierra highways for six weeks doing more surveys. They met with McCoy at Mammoth, but Hill ruled out Mammoth Mountain as a possible ski resort, calling it too wild and inaccessible.

Instead, Hill found what he considered the ideal spot in the Sierra for building a ski area: Mineral King, a magnificent, creek-hollowed valley on the range's western slope surrounded on three sides by high bowls usually buried in deep powder in winter. In addition to offering excellent ski terrain, Mineral King lay just outside of what was then the southern boundary of Sequoia National Park, accessible from San Francisco and only about 200 miles north of Los Angeles—a hundred miles closer than Mammoth. Hill wasn't alone. The following year, David Brower conducted a survey of the Sierra Nevada for the Sierra Club—which then favored building a new ski resort in the Sierra—and also settled on Mineral King as the best location.

"Corty Hill decided Mammoth wasn't a good place to build a ski area," McCoy recalls with a characteristic grin. "They said it was too far from a metropolitan area, it was too high in altitude, it was

Above: McCoy, skiing in his characteristic T shirt, always got satisfaction from enabling skiers to have a good time. Below: The family that skis together: Gary, Roma and Dave McCoy.

too remote from any road or town, there were no facilities. They said it wasn't what people were accustomed to—too much snow, too windy, too rugged. They said Mammoth could not be tamed... Mineral King was accessible by paved roads to the base, and they had a vision that they could put a train in to go to all of the good skiing areas there." After that, Hill's attention shifted from skiing in the Eastern Sierra to establishing a resort at Mineral King. Years afterward, Hill admitted his mistake: "I told Dave [McCoy] that every time I saw Mammoth Mountain, it was enveloped in storm clouds and that he would not have enough sunny days, there was too much snow. He knew better. He was right and I was wrong."

Undeterred by Hill's assessment, McCoy's attention stayed riveted on Mammoth Mountain. After years of doing hydrography surveys on the big mountain, he knew it better than anyone. He knew every arc and contour, where the snow piled up the highest and where it lingered the longest. McCoy knew the challenges the mountain's weather and location posed, but believed he could conquer them through ingenuity and hard work.

As the end of the 1940s neared, Dave drove a pregnant Roma to the mountain's north slope on a Weasel. She recalls, "Dave said, 'See that hill up there?' I looked up and couldn't see anything but trees. 'That's where I'm going to have my first chairlift,' he said." Meanwhile, Hans Georg, also unswayed by Hill's survey, continued nurturing his own dreams of building a first-class ski resort at Mammoth. He and McCoy remained neighborly, however. Redmon says that on a few occasions, McCoy sent him over to help Georg fix his tows.

In the meantime, the Forest Service had formed its own ideas about Mammoth Mountain's resort potential. In 1945, a forest ranger named Fred Meckel had written a report singling out Mammoth Mountain as the only spot in the Sierra south of Lake Tahoe worthy of a major capital investment to build a ski area. The same year that Hill did his survey, Jim Gibson gathered together a party that included Meckel, Georg and a few other Eastern Sierra

Alpenglow illuminates the Minarets above Ediza Lake deep in the Ansel Adams Wilderness.

Above, left: As the 1950s wore on, the fame of Mammoth Mountain's long, open slopes grew rapidly. Above right: The Snake Pit, covered by a relatively light snowfall.

Ski Club members for a series of ski tours across Mammoth Mountain to assess its possibilities. On the first trip, they climbed the southeast side of the mountain, crossed to the head of Dry Creek and then zigzagged down the canyon. The group returned for later trips to explore the north-facing slopes.

"Mammoth Mountain is impressive in its ski potentialities," Gibson wrote afterward in a report. "Long, open slopes on both north and south[east] sides of the mountain offer a great variety of terrain. It seems beyond any question that proper development can make this mountain one of the top ski areas of the West." He added that the ski slopes on the east side couldn't compare in quality to the north-facing ones, but also noted the north side's inaccessibility. Georg applied that year for a permit to install a chairlift on the east side, but Gibson recommended against it. Instead, he wrote that the Forest Service should build a new paved

Badge of honor: A Mammoth Mountain Ski Club patch.

road to the north side, where a ski resort with chairlifts and a first-class hotel should be built.

The agency's drive to develop a ski resort in the Eastern Sierra was spurred by the speedy growth of skiing in Southern California after World War II. The war brought a huge industrial boom to the Southland, particularly to the aviation industry that had sprouted there because of its perfect flying weather. The federal government

spent about $35 billion in California during World War II, and continued to fuel the Southern California economy during the decades of the Cold War. More skiers than ever before were traveling up Highway 395 from the prosperous Southland to ski the Eastern Sierra. "After the war, things picked up very fast," McCoy says. "People made good money in those days in industry, and they were looking for recreation. The aviation companies started their own ski clubs, and they had their own bus trips. We would have a hundred buses parked out here [at Mammoth] in the late '40s and '50s," McCoy says. Where hundreds of out-of-town skiers on the Eastern Sierra slopes had once impressed the local newspapers, by the early 1950s thousands were coming. Many of them were lobbying the Forest Service to bring a bona fide ski resort with chairlifts to the Eastern Sierra's superb skiing terrain.

To deal with the growing crowds, McCoy installed diesel engines in his tows for extra power, and they became known as the fastest in the country with the exception of those at Suicide Six in Vermont. McCoy's souped-up tows could move 1,800 skiers an hour, which was more than the capacity of Squaw Valley with its chairlift. Skiers were pulled by a sling that ran around their waists and attached to the rope, which they gripped with a nut-cracker-like handle. It took stamina just to hang onto them. "Those

rope tows were very long and very fast. You could always recognize Mammoth skiers by their long arms," Wolfgang Lert quips.

In 1952, the Forest Service started following up on its plans to establish a modern, full-service ski area on Mammoth Mountain. The agency started by building the new paved road to the north side that Gibson considered the key to Mammoth's future. Next, officials put out a prospectus with a closing date of April 30, 1953, seeking a developer with $250,000 to erect a European-style ski facility with a chairlift, a T-bar and a lodge on the north slope. McCoy certainly had no money to put up; he barely made enough from his hydrographer job and ski tows to support his family. Georg, meanwhile, had been bragging about his Hollywood connections and the wealthy friends he had backing him. McCoy says, "I thought somebody with money was going to come in and I'd be out in the cold. But I wasn't going to leave until they pushed me out."

Forest Service officials sat back for six months and waited to hear from prospective developers. They never received a single bid.

Above: Skiers motoring up from Southern California in the late '40s were greeted with a panoramic view of oversized Mammoth. Below: A McCoy family picnic on the Mountain.

In the 1950s, skiers took full advantage of the spacious sundecks on the newly built Main Lodge.

"People didn't think it was feasible because of that survey that Corty Hill, Hannes Schneider and the Forest Service did," McCoy explains. With no other bidders on the horizon, the agency came to McCoy with a proposition. "I didn't have the dollars to do what they asked," he recalls. "They turned that around and asked me what I could do. They made a prospectus out of that, and said, 'Go to work on it.'" For McCoy, it was the opportunity of a lifetime. The agency gave him a 25-year lease, and he agreed to build a chairlift on Mammoth's north side as fast as he could, and to add two more lifts after that. "We told them if they would give us a chance, we'd try to do what they asked as soon as possible," McCoy says. "We just took a piece of paper and drew in Lifts 1, 2 and 3, and we said we'd build them in a timely fashion, and they said okay."

The agency had its doubts, however. Redmon recalls, "The Forest Service said they didn't want to see Dave do too much, because they said it would never get off the ground. They thought it was going to be a short-term thing; it was not going to be any big resort."

Now it was Georg who was out in the cold, feeling frustrated and disappointed. It had always been obvious to the agency that

Right: For skiers, following the sun as it warms sucessive faces of the huge peak has been a Mammoth tradition for more than 50 years.

In this rare photo, the Snake Pit (center) and a concession stand next to it share the base area with the newly completed Main Lodge (right). This is still prior to the construction of Chair 1.

Georg would be harder to deal with than the hard-working, eager-to-please McCoy, and also that McCoy had a better chance of succeeding. Georg might be better at publicizing a resort, but some-one had to build it first. Rocky Rockwell, who worked for the Forest Service in Mammoth as a cultural resources specialist in the early '50s, commented, "The basic problem was Hans Georg's personality. If Hans had the personality Dave has, and the mechanical ability Dave has, the probability is that Dave McCoy might never have been on Mammoth Mountain. It would have been Hans Georg."

Upon sealing the deal with the Forest Service, McCoy quit his job of 18 years with the water department and set to work building a

Above, left: Before the snow piled up skiers had to sidestep up a steep ramp to load onto Chair 1. McCoy later solved that problem with an adjustable terminal. Above, right: Worker Tom Dempsey admires McCoy's homemade crane—a 45-foot telephone pole lashed onto a two-ton truck bed.

ski lodge. He and his men dug the foundation by hand, and they scrounged up cement, sand and gravel from McCoy's friends at the water department and the Mono County road-maintenance yard. When they were finished, a two-story wooden warming hut with a spacious lobby, fireplace, cafe, ski shop and a flat roof that doubled as a sundeck stood at the bottom of the mountain.

McCoy and his crew were preparing to build the first chairlift themselves, but fortuitously, a San Francisco company called United Tramway Engineers had just gone into the business of making chairlifts and had one unsold lift. Hearing about McCoy's new venture at Mammoth, the company offered him the double chairlift on credit, and also to help finance its installation. As soon as the snow melted in the spring of '55, McCoy and an expanded eight-man crew started assembling and installing the chairlift where the Broadway Express chairlift sits today. "They made the Erector set, and we put it up," McCoy remarks.

During the project, an engineer supplied by the lift company clashed with a 19-year-old kid named Tom Dempsey working for McCoy. Already unhappy with the engi-

Above: McCoy and his men used an ingenious portable cement mixer to set lift towers. Below: Ex-Seabee Bob Bumbaugh worked for McCoy at Mammoth Mountain for decades as an engineer and manager.

neer's approach, McCoy fired him and took over the tricky installation job himself. The men had to do the heavy work with a minimum of construction equipment, and what they had was mostly makeshift. McCoy built an A-frame into the bed of a two-ton six-by-six military supply truck and lashed a 45-foot telephone pole onto it to serve as a crane. They used that contraption, which had a tendency to tip over at inopportune times, to sink the massive lift towers.

The Southern California media closely tracked the progress of the construction and started a buzz in the Southland about the new chair. A month before it started operating, an article and large photo spread in the *Los Angeles Times* described the project, calling McCoy "an affable, good-looking guy in his early 40s, sort of a small edition of Paul Bunyan." Crediting him with "amazing inventiveness and ingenuity," it marveled that "he designed, on the spot, special tools, rigs and gimmicks to transport the 6,000-pound towers up the steep mountains for placement in the rock-hard ground."

In only three months, they erected a 3,500-foot-long, diesel-driven double chairlift with a vertical rise of 1,000 feet that

DAVE ON A WIRE

from "The Double Life of Dave McCoy" by Burton Hersh

It was late afternoon in mid-September and the regulars of the Mammoth Mountain trail crew were beginning to think they would have it made by sundown. But then the temporary line that was hauling the heavy main cable for the new chair lift separated and sent the cable snapping and rippling wildly from the tower assemblies. In disgust, the boys let the cable lie where it had fallen.

Just after daybreak the next morning the youthful-minded middle-aged man who developed and operates this huge

McCoy never asked his workers to do anything that he wasn't willing to do himself.

California area, Dave McCoy, roared up to the summit in his mufflerless jeep to see what could be done.

He had the line re-attached. He jockeyed a multi-tired brontosaurus of a crane into position below the topmost tower. Turning the crane over to his foreman, McCoy darted up the rungs of the tower, shimmied along the upper crossbar which was a hair-raising 50 feet above the abyss and straddled the rocker arm. He swung his foot out, caught the cable and lifted it over the wheel assembly. Then he skittered down.

At this point, one aghast spectator asked McCoy why he himself still did such dangerous work. "Cause I'm used to it," he said simply. "If you haven't done a lotta this kind of thing, the tendency's to try and put the cable on with your fingers up there. That's how you get your fingers snipped right off."

McCoy radioed his base crew, swung back into the cab of his crane and started on his zig-zagging course to the tower below. Nobody had come close to panic; but nobody had wasted any time either. Even in mid-September, at more than 11,000 feet in the central Sierra Nevada, the thunderheads thickening beyond the ragged northern peaks could mean feet of snow within a couple of hours. It was crucial that the cable be back in service by then. Characteristically, McCoy had taken whatever chances he felt to be necessary and had no interest in taking even a small one that had no bearing on the present problem. ❂

—*SKI* Magazine, December 1964

could carry 900 people an hour, then the largest capacity of any lift of its kind in California. "The speed and accuracy with which the construction progressed startled even those professionally in the tramway business," *The Times* noted.

McCoy was preparing the chair for a Thanksgiving Day 1955 grand opening, but not much snow had fallen that autumn and ski conditions were still marginal. As McCoy worked all through the night before Thanksgiving putting the finishing touches on the chair, he poked his head out of the freshly built lift shack and saw

Chair 1 lift towers ascend to a saddle above Gravy Chute and Broadway. The Main Lodge stands beside the road at the bottom of the hill.

Above, left: The media buzz in Southern California brought hundreds of skiers to Mammoth Mountain for the opening of Chair 1 on Thanksgiving Day, 1955.
Above, right: With hundreds waiting to ride the new chair, others elected to ride the rope tow (foreground).

that a light snow was beginning to fall. By morning, three feet of new snow had collected on the mountainside, and the sun was shining. A perfect ski morning greeted the thousands of skiers who had driven up Highway 395 from Southern California the day before and were now crowding behind the newly completed chair. Many had been attracted by the publicity about the new chairlift and were skiing Mammoth for the first time. They had jammed every lodge and motel in the Eastern Sierra; some overflow skiers were forced to stay in Mojave, 220 miles away.

McCoy stood on the wooden lift ramp and gave a short speech. The day was a dream come true for him, he said to assembled skiers, his voice breaking with emotion. When they fired up the lift, riding in the first two chairs were Roma McCoy and a teenage ski racer from Bishop named Jill Kinmont, whose tragic but inspirational story would eventually touch millions. Then, two by two, the lift began carrying the crowd of skiers up the mountain, ushering in a new era of Eastern Sierra skiing.

Rockwell says, "The chairlift was what made Mammoth. Prior to the chairlift, a lot of local people came to Mammoth,

Opposite: McCoy gazes up at a newly set Chair 1 lift tower in October, 1955, a month before the chair first started operating. He worked around the clock for days to ready it for the Thanksgiving Day opening.

Above: Roma McCoy (left) rode the first chair on opening day, along with paralyzed ski racer Jill Kinmont, being strapped in by Dave McCoy.

[and some regulars] came up from Southern California for skiing on rope tows. But the day the chairlift opened at Mammoth, a whole different crowd appeared—hundreds of people who'd never been there before, attracted by that chairlift. Mammoth has gone big time ever since. From that day on, I think it far exceeded what anybody thought."

Hans Georg never really recovered from seeing his Mammoth dream slip away. He continued operating his tows on the east side for a few years, but abandoned them soon after McCoy's first chairlift began running. McCoy allowed Georg to bring clients to his chairlifts and to work there as a ski instructor. However, Georg sank into depression and threatened suicide. His friends Joe and Opal Miller say he suffered a mental breakdown later in the 1950s and entered a mental asylum in Los Angeles. There, they say, he received numerous shock treatments that only worsened his mental and physical health. In the 1960s, he was well enough to return to Mammoth, where he lived in his isolated cabin with six cats and began teaching skiing again, but his friends say he was only a shell of his former self.

One snowy day in the mid 1960s, Georg suffered a heart attack at his cabin and died. No one came by the cabin to find his body for weeks. According to local legend, by the time someone did, they made a gruesome discovery: The starving cats shut in the closed house had begun eating his corpse. A Mammoth Lakes art show that Georg had started, a ski race and a ski trail on Mammoth Mountain were named for him after his death, but in recent years his name and memory have faded from Mammoth. ✪

Up close, Mammoth Mountain shows its incredible variety of terrain. The cone-shaped peak in the foreground is called Lincoln Mountain.

Previous page: The whole enchilada at sunset—Mammoth Mountain
(left), the Minarets (center) and Mount Ritter and Banner Peak (far
right). Above: A racer shaves a gate in the 1997 Women's World Cup
giant slalom at Mammoth.

chapter   5

Racing Days

Ski racing is so deeply ingrained in the history of Mammoth Mountain

that it turns up everywhere, like a geometric pattern in a Turkish rug.

Like almost everything about Mammoth, it begins with Dave McCoy.

A racer practically from the time he first strapped on skis, McCoy

evolved into a spectacularly successful racing coach, a guru to young

ski competitors. Unlike some ski resort owners who believed that

racing clashed with their real business of drawing recreational skiers,

he always had the welcome mat out for racers.

By the 1960s, Mammoth had become a ski racing mecca, a legendary training ground for young athletes from across the country. The mountain was definitely well suited for the role. It had the terrain for any kind of race, and the extra-long snow season that allowed racers to train in the off-season after other resorts had already shut down. McCoy was always accommodating, keeping the lifts running late for racers and frequently reaching into his own pocket to help them.

In 1974, McCoy started the first ski-area race department, a concept that soon spread to other resorts. Today, Mammoth Mountain's race department maintains a full-time staff that not only puts together major events like World Cup races and National Alpine Championships, but also provides state-of-the-art racing facilities and coaching for skiers and snowboarders, from kids to adults.

"Dave McCoy initiated the concept of amateurs racing on a professional-style course," says John Armstrong, former director of Mammoth Mountain's race department and now head of the resort's executive-training program. "Before that, ski-club groups of volunteers would come here [to Mammoth] and stage events on the mountain all by themselves. The ski area would assign them a trail, and they would unroll their timing equipment, their gates, and

Super G turns across Cornice Bowl. Mammoth is one of only a handful of ski resorts in the U.S. that have the terrain and the willingness to host World Cup races.

would attempt to put on the race on an amateur basis. Sometimes it went very well, sometimes rather poorly."

Seeing this and deciding they would be better off doing things right, McCoy offered Mammoth's services, including professional course layout, timing equipment, officiating and expert race coaching. It turned out to be an opportunity that skiers really coveted, as the next few decades proved. Adult weekend warriors loved the chance to race a professional-style course where they might outski their friends or coworkers, and kids also thrived on the competition. At the same time, it turned out to be a very healthy idea for the resort. Once it started up, word about Mammoth's racing program quickly spread through Southern California ski clubs and other organizations, and the extra ski trips it attracted boosted Mammoth's skier numbers handsomely. That

Badge of the Far West Ski Association.

interest may have peaked a few years back, but it remains popular. In 2001, Mammoth Mountain held 50,000 racing starts.

As fine a racing instructor as McCoy was, tragic events in the mid 1950s almost ended his coaching career before it started. McCoy had always allowed high school kids from the valley town of Bishop to assist him with his rope-tow operations, taking tickets or carrying gas cans in exchange for skiing privileges, kids like Charlotte Zumstein who won the 1949 Junior Nationals. They learned to ski from Toni Milici, one of McCoy's regular work crew who earned a living as a ski instructor, first at McGee and then at Mammoth. In the early '50s, McCoy was busy with construction projects during the summers but had free time in winter, so he took over the coaching of any of Milici's young students who showed exceptional skiing ability and wanted to learn how to race. The very best of them, the ones who were the most

Above, left: Winning smiles. Left to right, young ski racers Gary McCoy, Dennis Agee, Craig Holiday, Greg Moore and Pat Cooper show off their trophies. Above, right: Dave McCoy kneels in front of his young racers at a Sun Valley competition in the early '50s. Jill Kinmont is at far right, Gary McCoy is third from right and Jill's brother Bobby is fourth from right.

serious about training and learning to become top ski racers, McCoy invited to sleep on the living room floor in his Crowley Lake house on weekends so that they could be closer to the ski slopes. Among them were three Bishop teens named Jill Kinmont (now Boothe), Kenny Lloyd and Linda Meyers (now Tikalsky).

McCoy was a role model to the kids, and they called him "Pa." Kinmont, a pretty, blue-eyed blond, quickly showed phenomenal skiing talent. At 15 years old, she was the all-American girl: sweet, modest and appealingly down-to-earth, but at the same time a fiery competitor. Kinmont Boothe remembers, "It was extremely special to be able to stay over on Saturday night at their place. It was just kind of a legend at the high school that you were really 'in' if you got to be one of those that stayed over, so when that moment came, I felt I had arrived."

McCoy turned out to have an amazing talent for training young racers. He had uncanny instincts for analyzing skiing ability and a knack for connecting with individual skiers at their own level. He was firm, without being a drill instructor. McCoy knew when to encourage athletes if they lacked confidence, to gently rein them in if they needed it, or to just leave them alone.

Future Olympian Linda Meyers does dryland training while Coach McCoy and Jill Kinmont look on.

"He would pick out something you did right and then point that out and indicate that if you just did that all the time, there's nobody that could touch you," Kinmont Boothe recalls.

McCoy trained his athletes hard in the usual ways, having them ski and run slalom gates repeatedly for hours on end, and do dryland exercises such as running through tires to develop quickness and agility. The fun-loving McCoy, however, also made training enjoyable for kids by inventing his own imaginative teaching techniques.

Linda Meyers Tikalsky recalls, "He taught us how to prejump at his house," referring to the practice of jumping ahead of a bump on a course to maintain control. "He had Kenny Lloyd and Jill and me jumping from one piece of furniture in the living room to another. Two jumps on the couch and then another jump to a chair and then another jump to a rocker, to teach us how to lift and get our weight up and forward. It probably didn't do the furniture any good, but Roma didn't say a word."

In 1964, McCoy explained one of his training exercises to a writer for *SKI* Magazine. He had a team of racers unloading a truck full of watermelons, standing in a line and passing the melons

Above, left and right: By the mid 1950s, Jill Kinmont was probably the top female skier in the United States.

along. "They don't lift or throw the thing," McCoy explained. "They get a pushing rhythm where the weight is carried rapidly along. Each person barely carries the weight of the melon. That's the way we translate this to skiing. Skiing is a sensitive touch of the snow. You carry your weight down the hill with a light touch to change its direction, rather than a severe, continuous turning moment. If it's explained right, kids seek this light, fluid movement on the snow."

Although several of McCoy's young racers of the early '50s showed obvious ability, no one could touch Jill Kinmont. She copied McCoy's elegant, graceful skiing style and drove it with her own fearless determination. Milici recalls one day in the early 1950s when he was skiing with Kinmont at Mammoth. "She was standing up at the top of the Number 2 rope tow, and it was all moguls, real hard," he says. "I hollered, 'Jill! Schuss it!'" She knew Milici was only joking, but the mischievous Kinmont gazed downhill, went into a tuck and rocketed straight through the mogul field.

"All I could say was, 'Jesus Christ!' She was that good," Milici says. In 1953, Jill won enough races to represent the Far West Ski Association at the Junior National Championships. The

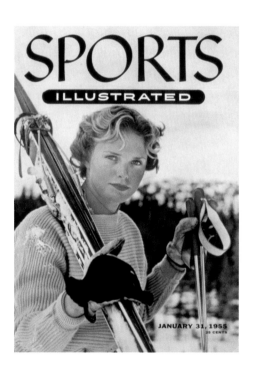

Kinmont appeared on the cover of *Sports Illustrated* the week of her tragic accident.

next year, she captured first place in the slalom event at the Junior National Championships at Jackson Hole, then followed that by winning the slalom at the U.S. National Championships at Aspen, becoming the first person ever to hold both titles at the same time. Back home in Bishop, the local chamber of commerce, Lions and Kiwanis collected money to help finance hometown girl Kinmont's racing career.

At the dawn of 1955, Kinmont was probably the top female ski racer in the United States, and her beauty and vivacious personality were making her a celebrity. Coaches and ski writers considered her a shoo-in to make the 1956 Olympic team. One of the last big races before the Olympic trials in March 1955 was the Snow Cup in Alta, Utah, where most of the Olympic hopefuls would be competing. Just before the race, the January 31 issue of *Sports Illustrated* appeared on the newsstands, its cover a close-up color portrait of 18-year-old Kinmont looking more like an outdoorsy young Hollywood starlet than an athlete. Inside, Jill was the subject of more photos and a cover story, "Apple Pie in Sun Valley," with the subheading, "Pretty Skier Aims for Olympics."

The former ski racer has sold every painting she has put up for sale in the last four years. In "Canal Headgate," (above), she used muted colors to depict an Owens Valley scene.

chronicled her life and injury, according to Larsen.

"At first, I thought that her paintings sold just because she was Jill Kinmont of *The Other Side of the Mountain* fame," says Larsen, who used to display Jill's paintings in the arts council's gallery on Bishop's Main Street. "But when the watercolors were hanging in our gallery, I noticed that people who didn't

"In 1960, he had [ski manufacturer] Kneissl make me skis without a groove," Meyers Tikalsky says. "Fifteen to 20 years later, they started making skis without a groove. He worked on the edges of skis in the mid '50s, long before anybody else did that. He filed them and put a burr on them to make them hold better on hard snow. His method of taking care of skis and waxing skis was far advanced, and he taught us all how to do it."

McCoy was also an expert racing tactician, Meyers Tikalsky says. "One of the things that he could do really well was pick a line [through a slalom course]. Dave developed a line where you entered the gate at a higher point and went straighter for a greater distance," which made for faster finishes. In coaching as in everything else, McCoy was a maverick who did things his own way. *SKIING* Magazine reported in the '60s, "McCoy has aroused envy in the ranks of some of the coaches, mostly for the way in which young skiers respond to him. It's a natural envy, compounded by the great success McCoy has had."

Dennis Agee, who learned to race from McCoy and sandwiched two stints as coach of the U.S. Ski Team in between working at Mammoth, believes that McCoy's success was keyed to his sturdy personality. "The thing that attracted those athletes was that Dave was extremely consistent as a coach, which is very important. You could just count on him all the time. He was solid as a rock." Agee says that he based his own coaching style on what he learned from McCoy. "After having been coached by him,

Above: U.S. Ski Team Coach Bob Beattie (right) stands with the 1966 Womens' World Championship Team, all of whom were trained at Mammoth. Left to right: Wendy Allen, Suzy Chaffee, Jean Saubert, Cathy Allen, Joan Hannah and Penny McCoy. Below: Future U.S. Ski Team coach Dennis Agee, running slalom gates in the 1960s, learned to race and to coach from Dave McCoy.

I learned to make sure that you're understanding each individual. You're not just coaching to a group, doing a cookie-cutter presentation where one statement or one observation fits all." One of McCoy's faults as a coach, however, was his refusal to involve himself in the politics and gamesmanship that inevitably accompanied ski racing at the highest levels, which became more important in advancing a skier's career as the sport grew. "He felt that results should speak for themselves; you shouldn't have to go and negotiate afterward," one ski racing expert says.

By the late 1950s, some of the biggest stars in international skiing started gravitating to Mammoth. Austrian ski team member Anderl Molterer, who won silver and bronze medals at the 1956 Winter Olympics, came to Mammoth to train and asked McCoy for help with his technique. Christian Pravda, who won silver and bronze skiing medals at the 1952 Games, also spent a lot of time at Mammoth and became a good friend of McCoy's. French ski racer Jean-Claude Killy and Austrian Karl Schranz were among the star athletes who breezed through Mammoth in the 1960s. Partly

Lake Mary in the Mammoth Lakes basin serves as a reflecting pool for the back side of Mammoth Mountain.

1960s, and Penny McCoy made the U.S. Ski Team later in the '60s.

Gary and Penny might have excelled even more had they been given more opportunity. Gary McCoy never made a U.S. Olympic team, even though many believe he should have. "Gary was certainly an outstanding natural talent and one of the best slalom and GS skiers in the country, recognized by the Europeans as one of the major threats from the U.S. But he was not selected for the national team," says Mammoth's former race department head John Armstrong. Penny's bronze medal at the 1966 FIS World Championships at Portillo, Chile, was the only medal captured by the U.S. at the competition. She was named to the 1968 Olympic squad but was arbitrarily moved off the team along with another skier at the last minute by U.S. Ski Team coach Bob Beattie, Meyers Tikalsky says. Some who remember the incidents believe that Beattie, who coached the U.S. team from 1961 to 1969, rebuffed the McCoy kids at least partly because of irritation over the way they had been trained, while others say it was jealousy over their father's coaching success. Beattie's authoritarian manner and grueling training regimen certainly clashed with Dave McCoy's low-key, intuitive approach. "He just bypassed [Gary], it didn't have anything to do with following the rules or putting on the guy with the most points," Meyers Tikalsky says of Beattie. "What happened with Penny was the final blow." By the end of the 1960s, Dave

Among the racing McCoy kids, Poncho and Penny's achievements stood out.

Opposite: Dave McCoy with his racing offspring, left to right, Penny, Poncho and Gary.

Above: Penny McCoy (left) stands on the podium at Portillo, Chile after taking the bronze medal at the 1966 FIS World Championships. Below: Poncho, running gates in a Far West Ski Association race, was a top downhiller who made the U.S. Olympic Team.

Above: The Minarets provide a stunning backdrop for racing. Below: Spectators gathered at the bottom of Mammoth Mountain to watch 1994 Women's World Cup events.

McCoy, who was never asked to coach a national team despite his years of success, retired from serious coaching and concentrated on building his ski area.

Beattie dismisses the flap, pointing to the medals won by Jimmie Heuga and Billy Kidd at the 1964 Innsbruck Olympics. "I wasn't running for a popularity contest," Beattie says. "The kids made the team or didn't make the team based on their results, period. The record speaks for itself." Even though Beattie and Dave McCoy have forged a good relationship in the years since then, the former Olympic team coach remains a highly controversial figure at Mammoth Mountain.

Mammoth's race department is still considered the nation's best. The resort hosted several FIS World Cup women's slalom and

Opposite: Carrie Sheinberg of the U.S. Ski Team in the 1994 Women's World Cup slalom held on Mammoth's Fascination run.

Alpine snowboard racing (above, left) and boardercross (above, right) were added to the Mammoth Mountain competition mix in the late '90s.

Super G races in the 1990s. Only a few other U.S. resorts have the terrain to satisfy the strict FIS course specifications for length, steepness and location on the mountain for the World Cup. And not all of them want to host the expensive races. Mammoth had to divert 250 employees to work on the last World Cup races it hosted, and the total price tag hovered around $750,000, Armstrong says. Preparing the course can take as long as a month, and large sections of the mountain have to be closed off. Mammoth technicians were up at 4:00 a.m. on race day, icing down trails, putting the finishing touches on 40,000 feet of fencing, and stringing and burying 60,000 feet of television cable, which extended from the Mammoth Mountain Inn parking lot to the Cornice at the summit, so that the start could be televised. In addition to the technical on-mountain work, lodging, catering, media facilities and other services provided by the resort, many Mammoth locals of Italian, French, German or other national origin

The Cornice Bowl start launches racers onto sweeping turns on wide-open slopes.

volunteer to act as liaisons, hosts and interpreters for foreign skiers.

The mountain also regularly hosts FIS Development Series races for 16- to 25-year-olds who are trying to improve their international rankings to make the U.S. Ski Team.

"Fascination and Far West are our two primary race runs," Armstrong explained to a *SKI* Magazine writer. "In 1988, Dave gave us the go-ahead to tear out an old T-bar and bulldoze a really fine race pitch. He had us name it Far West in honor of our Ski Association competition division. That summer of 1988 we also put in a new chair to serve the race hills, a new timing shack, two new video rooms and a public-address room. All this cost us a couple million dollars, but Dave saw it as a good investment for our racers."

Along with the variety of other competitions held each year at Mammoth, the resort has hosted the U.S. Ski and Snowboard Association (USSA) Grand Prix snowboard events, which include halfpipe and gate-running competitions.

McCoy's tradition of training young racers continues today in Mammoth's USSA-affiliated junior racing program, for kids who want to advance as competitive skiers or snowboarders. Fifteen full-time and 15 part-time Mammoth coaches instruct the juniors, who spend up to six days a week learning to compete on-mountain or sometimes training in the weight room. The roughly 200 youngsters in the program are mostly Mammoth locals, but include some who come up

Renowned snowboarder Rob Kingwill trained at Mammoth for the 2001 Gravity Games half pipe competition.

from Southern California and stay with families in town. Mammoth Lakes attorney Tim Sanford's son Adam started as a junior racer when he was seven years old, and his other son, Seth, started as a Mighty Mite when he was five. "Mammoth Mountain's kids' race teams are excellent," Sanford says. "The coaches take it very seriously, but they like little kids. They always act appropriately; they aren't just like Nazi coaches out there pushing the kids too hard."

Mammoth remains a big favorite of the Southern California ski club leagues affiliated with the Far West Ski Association. The Los Angeles Council of Ski Clubs' two racing leagues, Rokka and Ullr, and the Orange Council of Ski Clubs' Schusski league, frequently hold their races at Mammoth Mountain, a tradition that

ANDREA MEAD LAWRENCE

On the cold, gray day of the women's slalom at the 1952 Winter Olympics in Oslo, Norway, the course was so icy that Andrea Mead Lawrence could see leaves and sticks beneath the frozen surface as if they were embedded in Plexiglas. The 19-year-old ski racer was sailing through the first run when she caught a tip on a gate and spun off the course. Instead of quitting, she scrambled back up to the gate and ripped through the rest of the run. Then she skied so fast in the second run that she made up more than four seconds and took the gold medal. Four decades later, veteran Olympic chronicler Bud Greenspan was still calling it "the most incredible moment in the history of winter sports." The Olympian herself later called it the defining moment of her life.

Andrea Mead Lawrence became a four-term county supervisor from Mammoth Lakes known for her tough stands on environmental and town planning issues.

She ended up taking a second gold medal in giant slalom in Oslo, and is still the only American skier to capture two golds at a single Olympic Games. Lawrence was recognized as the best female skier in the world in the early '50s, rarely losing a ski race between 1951 and 1955. In addition to her Olympic victories, she took three U.S. National Championships and won the Arlberg-Kandahar slalom and many other major international races in Austria, Switzerland and Italy, as well as the Harriman Cup at Sun Valley.

Lawrence grew up in Vermont, where her parents started the Pico Peak ski area, and she learned to ski around the time she learned to walk. After her racing career ended following the '56 Olympics, she moved to Aspen, where she lived for several years with her husband, David Lawrence, and their five children. She moved to Mammoth in 1968 and fairly quickly made a big impression—and not because she was a ski celebrity.

The ski racing star came to Mammoth Lakes just around the time that the town's first zoning plan went into effect. She had served on the planning commission in Aspen, and paid attention when a developer turned up in Mammoth asking for a zoning change to build a series of eight-story condominiums at the foot of Mammoth Mountain. The condos were ridiculously out of proportion in the little town, where a three-story building was a skyscraper. When the county planning commissioner green-lighted the high-rise project anyway, several locals asked Lawrence to head a new community group called "Friends of Mammoth" to fight it and she accepted. Lawrence says, "When an idea has its moment in time, everything and everyone that has a role to play comes together. And that's what happened."

The group went to court to block the project, eventually carrying it to the California Supreme Court, while the developer began laying in the foundation for the condos. The work came to a halt when the state's high court decided in favor of Friends of Mammoth in a blockbuster, landmark decision. The case expanded the scope of a recently passed state law, requiring environmental impact reports to be written for developments on private land as well as for public projects. California lawyers still frequently cite the "Friends of Mammoth" case in court, and consider it the leading case in how the key California Environmental Quality Act is to be interpreted. Finally, the developer abandoned the foundation its crews had started digging, and the high-rises were never built.

Well respected in Mammoth Lakes following that victory, Lawrence decided to run for Mono County Supervisor in the district representing the town. She won and began the first of four terms as supervisor in 1983. While on the board of supervisors, Lawrence was known for her toughness and courageous stands of principle, as well as her deft political sense. Even though she often took strong positions on preserving the environment in a conservative rural county, she never lost an election. Lawrence supported the Mono Lake Committee and now serves on its board of directors, and also worked to protect the Bodie historical site.

Finally, in the late 1990s, as she retired from public life, she bookended her political career with another battle over building in

In the early '50s, Lawrence turned the ski racing world upside down by consistently defeating the Europeans. She is still the only American skier to capture two ski racing gold medals at a single Olympics.

Mammoth Lakes, this time with the town government. After the Intrawest Corp. had bought a share of Mammoth Mountain, the town filed a redevelopment plan to construct parking facilities and make other improvements in support of the corporation's planned development. Lawrence was disturbed by what she called a taxpayer rip-off, and resurrected the Friends of Mammoth with a few other concerned locals. "It's a reverse Robin Hood, taking from the poor to give to the rich," she said at the time. The group filed two lawsuits against the redevelopment plan, and even after the town prevailed in both of them, Lawrence was undeterred. "I have no question that they're going to lose at the appellate level," she said in 1998. She was right. The appeals court found in favor of the Friends of Mammoth, and the redevelopment plan was finally scrapped.

In 2002, Bud Greenspan put together a list of the top 10 greatest Winter Olympians of all time. The criteria included not only the athlete's achievements at the Olympic Games, but also factored in what they went on to accomplish in life after their Olympic careers ended. Sifting through the hundreds of top Olympic medalists for the final list, which included figure skating legends Sonja Henie and Dick Button and French skiing star Jean-Claude Killy, he ranked Andrea Mead Lawrence number one. ✪

goes back to Eastern Sierra skiing's earliest days.

"I can do a race clinic at Mammoth, like I did last March, and get some really good instruction, some wonderful information in a relatively small amount of time," says Maxine Hanlon, an officer of the Balboa Ski and Sports Club in Orange County. "I love going through a good course, and Mammoth sets very good courses."

Mammoth Mountain has also been a frequent host of USSA National Masters races, often highly competitive events for racers over the age of 25. Dave McCoy became active as a masters racer in the 1970s and 1980s, and capped his ski racing career by winning a national championship title in his class when he was in his mid 60s. ✪

Previous page: Despite recent growth in and around Mammoth Lakes, most parts of the area still look wild. Above: Dave McCoy's ingenuity and insistence on quality grooming has given Mammoth a well-deserved reputation for smooth snow surfaces.

Inventing Mammoth

When Dave McCoy inaugurated Mammoth's first chairlift in 1955 and raised the price of a daily lift ticket from $2.50 to $4, some of his crew thought he was taking a big chance. "We were worried that the $4 lift ticket would discourage some folks, but still they came," Toni Milici says. They certainly did. Business at Mammoth Mountain jumped 300 percent the first year the chairlift was running, from about 20,000 skiers in '54–'55 to 60,000 the following season. The new chairlift touched off a surge of popularity that would continue for the next three decades.

McCoy still had a few bugs to iron out of the new chair after it started running. "I think it took at least two or three people in the control tower to operate Chair 1," Don Redmon later told a Mammoth Lakes newspaper. "One guy to release the brake, another guy to pull something else and a third guy to push one button or something. It was hilarious. We operated that way for a day or two until Dave found out what the problems were." After that, the sheaves—the rubber-lined wheels that the cable ran on—kept wearing out. "Redmon and [Bob] Bumbaugh became so proficient at changing the sheaves that they could go up the tower, change the sheave and restart the lift in four minutes," the newspaper said. "Around

450 sheaves were changed the first season. The wheels for the cable were redesigned the following summer."

The steady increase in Mammoth's skier numbers over the next few seasons dovetailed perfectly with the plan McCoy had given the Forest Service to build two more chairlifts. There wasn't much question about what people wanted. McCoy was still operating his rope tows, but 75 percent of the skiers opted to use the chair. In 1957, he and his crew installed Chair 2, a 4,100-foot-long lift with a 900-foot vertical drop and 900-skiers-per-hour capacity, which was engineered by the Riblet Tramway Co. of Spokane, Washington. He borrowed from a local bank to finance the chair, one of a long series of short-term bank loans he received and paid back over the years. The summer before it opened, McCoy and company cut new trails through the pines, and skiers could now hurtle down runs named St. Moritz, Blue Ox, Powder Bowl and Fascination. The following summer, builders broke ground on a hotel at the base of Mammoth Mountain, easing one of the resort's biggest remaining problems.

As the *New York Herald Examiner* pointed out in an article about the new hotel, "almost unknown 10 years ago, Mammoth Mountain's fame has spread because of its fine skiing conditions seven months of the year." But, the article continued, "the nearest overnight lodging is five miles away, and on weekends it has been impossible for some to get rooms closer than 50 miles away." The 85-room hotel that finally changed that opened in December 1958 with much hoopla, reeling in media stars and VIPs from Southern California.

Above: McCoy's crew members Don Redmon (left) and Bob Bumbaugh (right) worked with him to install Chair 2, engineered by the Riblet Tramway Co. Below: McCoy's trusty crew at work.

Mammoth was rapidly becoming famous at the end of the 1950s, aided greatly by McCoy's ski coaching success. Kenny Lloyd would capture a race at Squaw Valley or Linda Meyers would take one in Switzerland, to say nothing of the frequent triumphs of the McCoy kids that soon followed. As those confident young racers continued to excel, people across the United States and Europe started wondering who this Dave McCoy was, and what was this Mammoth Mountain they kept

hearing about? Reporters wondered the same thing, and once they found out, they started writing stories proclaiming Mammoth to be the West's hottest new skiing spot.

The mushrooming crowds that followed continually outstripped the resort's capacity, and McCoy started building a new chairlift every few years to accommodate the throngs of new skiers.

He built Chair 3 in 1959, a 2,800-foot-long lift with a vertical rise of 1,000 feet, the first one to access the upper part of the mountain. It ran to the top of a central knob above a series of cascading bowls, opening up a broad wedge of fresh terrain. McCoy hired a new head ski instructor, Gus Weber, a Swiss ex-ski racer who came to Mammoth from Mont Tremblant in Canada. Leading the ski patrol was Marc Zumstein, a local skier whose daughter Charlotte had become a junior champion under McCoy's coaching. Unlike some ski area operators who were frequently at odds with their Forest Service landlords, McCoy maintained an excellent, cooperative relationship with them that continued for decades.

When Southern Californians were lured to Mammoth for the first time, they were often rewarded with some of the best skiing they had ever encountered. McCoy worked day, night and early morning to insure that skiers got the most out of his mountain. He became a pioneer of hill grooming, the now-standard art of packing and shaping snow to make skiing easier and less hazardous. Bumbaugh, who worked for McCoy for decades as an engineer and manager, told an interviewer in the mid 1970s that "a lot of other areas had the attitude that the way it falls is the way you ski it. We developed some of the snow grooming equipment that the industry uses today. You look at what you have to do, like

Opposite: Then, as now, deep powder lured good skiers to Mammoth. Here, Silver Chesak drops down the Shaft on Lincoln Mountain.

bumps to be smoothed, and you take whatever steel you can lay your hands on and you get out your welding torch.

"When the snow was thin down on the lower slopes, we'd move the portables up under the Cornice, and ski up there. Then we found out we could move snow from one place to another, either with a dozer blade or hauling it. We made various drags, ran hydraulics in between them so we could lift the blades independent of one another. Started spoiling our customers," he said.

McCoy added his own twists to what others had done, devising new ways to flatten and reshape snow to improve skiing. "We made the first tiller as far as I know, but we never thought anything about it," McCoy says. "We just applied farming ideas to snow, and called it snow farming. Churning it up, leveling it off, compacting it. We found better ways to do it with rotating harrows and long frames like a land leveler and pulled it with a snowcat. We had a couple of long bars and two or three different blades and a rotating wheel. Then we put a power unit on it and ran three rototiller-type [blades]. We made drags and huge rollers six feet in diameter to roll the snow in the spring and squeeze the water out

Above: As part of his early, innovative snow-grooming effort, McCoy dragged rollers behind snowcats to flatten the snow. Below: Skiers in the spring of 1969 sidestepped up the ramp to load onto Chair 1.

of it. We did it to make skiing better, make it easier, more fun."

Over the years, McCoy also did much to advance ski lift technology. He is credited with devising the simple yet at the time revolutionary concept of building lift towers that were adjustable. Ski lifts have to keep running in anything from a few inches of snow to 20 feet. To accommodate the difference, Mammoth's Chair 1, for example, was originally built with a long, high wooden access ramp. When there was less snowfall in the early season, skiers had to sidestep awkwardly up the ramp to get to the chairs. McCoy came up with the idea of building adjustable towers so that the

chairs could be raised or lowered according to snow levels, and worked with ski lift engineers to develop them. It was another one of his innovations that became an industry standard.

Mammoth's fame was spreading at the perfect time. In the mid 1950s, Alex Cushing, owner of Squaw Valley a few hundred miles to the north, had pulled off an amazing coup. Mainly through his smooth salesmanship, his little ski area on the back side of Lake Tahoe beat out Aspen, Sun Valley and Lake Placid among U.S. resorts to secure the first Winter Olympics to be held in the country in 28 years. The 1960 Squaw Valley Olympics was the first ever to be televised daily in the United States. National attention was riveted on the Games, and the U.S. teams performed well, taking three gold, four silver and three bronze medals. Penny Pitou took silvers for the U.S. in the women's downhill and giant slalom, and Betsy Snite added a slalom silver. (Linda Meyers was expected to medal but fell and broke her collarbone in the women's giant slalom, taking her out of the competition.)

Following the Olympics, interest in skiing exploded in the United States, just as it had after the 1932 Lake Placid Games. Tens of thousands of Americans who had never skied before were inspired to go out and try the sport. The Olympics focused international attention on the Sierra Nevada, and brought thousands of new skiers from Southern California swarming to Mammoth. McCoy was as methodical as ever, building new lifts and other facilities to keep up with the demand. He certainly had plenty of mountain to work with: He had barely even started to open up the huge north side.

Between 1962 and 1965, he added three new chairlifts, a T-bar and a new on-hill ski lodge called the Mid-Chalet. Over the

next two years, he spent $1 million to add a two-stage gondola, with the second leg climbing to the mountain summit near the Cornice Bowl. In 1967, the *Los Angeles Times* reported that Mammoth's skier visits had zoomed from 88,760 in 1955 to 327,000 in 1965. The resort's net sales leaped from $167,262 in 1955 to $1,023,545 in 1960, and approached $2 million by 1966. McCoy often says that whatever money he made, he always plowed most of it back into developing his ski resort.

"By the late 1950s, everybody working at Mammoth was drawing a salary except me," he laughs. "I never knew what I was going to get. I had enough to live on, that was all I cared about. I never took anything I didn't have to take; I put all of it back into the mountain."

Along with skiing's new chic and Mammoth's burgeoning popularity came offers from big-money resort operators. Animation and vacation-resort king Walt Disney, a devotee of downhill skiing who had helped develop Sugar Bowl and stage the Squaw Valley

Above: Mammoth, 1969. While some skiers take a break outside the Mid-Chalet (in the background), others catch a ride on Chair 3. Below: The two-stage gondola, completed in 1967, gave Mammoth skiers a comfortable lift to the summit.

THE GARAGE

To build chairlifts and other machinery for his Mammoth Mountain operation and keep it all running smoothly, Dave McCoy built a garage near Chair 1 and the Main Lodge. There he and his ex-Seabee friend Bob Bumbaugh, who was part of McCoy's Mammoth work crew almost from the beginning, also assembled some of the snow tillers and other grooming devices that were later widely adopted by the ski industry. In the early 1970s, McCoy replaced that garage with a much larger and more elaborate one that stands down the road, in between the Main Lodge and town. Even though the facility doesn't get much attention, its engineers and mechanics do some remarkable work there. In addition to maintaining the resort's sizable fleet of trucks, shuttle buses, snowcats and heavy equipment, the garage houses a fully equipped machine shop that its employees say is the biggest one between Reno and Los Angeles.

Over the years the garage provided a place for McCoy to express the deep interest in mechanical design that he had since he was a boy. He was able to experiment and innovate, improving on equipment that was on the market but didn't work the way he wanted it to. Craig Taylor, who runs the garage's vehicle maintenance shop, says, "Dave McCoy had a lot of confidence, and if someone out there didn't build something, he wanted to build it himself. He was always wanting to develop something innovative, and Bumbaugh was in the same trend."

What can they make in the garage's machine and fabrication shops?

"Anything you want," says Charles "Chic" Gladding, who runs the two shops. "If you can come up with the idea, we can make it." The shops have proved that over the years. Gladding is an Aussie who came to Mammoth by way of England, where he worked for the famed Cosworth Engineering, building racing engines for Jackie Stewart, François Cevert and other Formula One drivers. In addition to maintaining lifts and other machinery for the ski area, his shops take on special jobs, designing and constructing almost any part, covering or decoration out of metal, fiberglass, plastic, or other material. Their projects have ranged from large, complex ones such as building a giant crane specially designed to move over snow or through mud, to simpler ones like tweaking Dave McCoy's mountain and motocross bikes or hand-beating decorative steel grapevines for his son Gary's house. The shops are equipped with an oil-filled lathe that can

In addition to its primary purpose as a facility for building and maintaining his ski operation, McCoy used the garage he built at Mammoth Mountain to develop his interest in mechanical innovation.

turn gigantic slabs of metal, a shear that can cut half-inch plate steel, and a metal brake that can bend steel up to 16 feet long by one inch thick.

Among the shops' most impressive projects was one that Gladding undertook for McCoy in the early 1980s: building a prototype snowcat from scratch. The machine, sometimes called the "proto-cat," was much more powerful and could climb better than the snowcats that were on the market at the time. "It was something that Dave had always wanted to do," Gladding says. "We were having trouble getting the snowcats to do the job, and we had purchased some snowcats that were a real problem for us."

So Mammoth Mountain built its own model. "We manufactured all the parts for it—the cab, the control system, the chassis, the suspension. There's still not a machine out there with independent suspension like this had. We used it for a year. It climbed some pretty unbelievable places," Gladding says. The proto-cat had some correctable design flaws, like a cab that was hard to see from, but in the meantime snowcat manufacturers caught up with McCoy and improved their vehicles. Mammoth Mountain abandoned its prototype, and finally cut it up for scrap.

Welders in the garage's fabrication shop work on a new rail called The Colossus destined for the Unbound Terrain Park.

In winter, the garage stays open seven days a week, 20 hours a day, and sometimes 24 hours. Its vehicle department houses a complete shop for maintaining the resort's 31 shuttle buses, 100 or so licensed cars, trucks and vans, and array of heavy equipment—cranes, loaders, concrete mixers and the dump trucks that are changed into snowplows in winter. Also cared for and sometimes modified (some, for example, have been fitted with forklifts) in the garage are Mammoth and June Mountain's 40 snowcats. In addition to slope grooming, they're used for lift maintenance and occasional projects like Hollywood film shoots. The garage crew also takes care of the resort's portable snowmakers with a mounted fan gun that can pour out an acre-foot of snow in an hour, according to the snowcat maintenance manager John Walline.

McCoy still often stops by the shop to try out new concepts. Gladding says, "Any time either one of us comes up with a bright idea, we talk to each other about it." When he took a break for a recent interview, the engineer was in the middle of working with McCoy on the design of a new transportation idea. "I can't tell you about that one, but you'll be hearing about it soon," Gladding says. ✪

Diehard skiers on Chair 23 ride to the summit as a storm bears down on Mammoth Mountain.

Olympics, was keenly interested in further expanding his empire into the ski business in the early '60s. He made more than one offer to buy Mammoth Mountain, but McCoy turned them down, and Disney had to look elsewhere. Barron Hilton of the hotel chain tried to buy the resort, and according to Mammoth insiders, Lew Wasserman of MCA, then owner of Universal Studios, offered McCoy a tremendous sum for Mammoth in the 1970s. McCoy rejected those propositions as well.

While Mammoth Mountain was expanding, the town of Mammoth Lakes was also growing. The town swelled from 200 full-time residents at the end of the '50s to close to a thousand 10 years later. A few new lodges that had sprouted in town remained open during the winter, and the Mammoth Tavern was joined by a couple of new night spots such as the Christiana, which stayed hip in the '60s by featuring go-go dancers. Seeing the skiing boom as an opportunity, developers began building condominiums in Mammoth, sparking a move by prominent locals to pass the town's first building codes.

Bob Stanford, who owned the Tamarack Lodge in the Lakes Basin and became a county supervisor in the late '70s, says, "People were buying private land in other parts of California and then trading it to the Forest Service for sections of land in Mammoth to

Left: Dave Schemenauer rides "Dave's Wave" on the backside of Mammoth Mountain en route to the "Hole in the Wall," an often-skied natural rock tunnel.

Above, left: Following a 1959 snowstorm, crews dug Mammoth's first chairlift out by hand. Above, right: In 1969, tunnels had to be dug for Chair 1.

develop. We who lived here were concerned. Not all of the people who came in here were very responsible developers. [A committee formed by the county] worked for five or six years on trying to get some building codes in here to prevent trashy buildings from being built and to try to control irresponsible developers."

No one aided the budding community more than Dave McCoy. He bought property at the base of Mammoth Mountain, although he was never interested in developing it himself. "I'll build the mountain, you build the town," was his motto. "I bought a lot of little properties, and I gave most of them away," McCoy says. "I figured that someday there would have to be something done in town. I'm not a developer: I bought property and kept it out of circulation."

In the earlier days when the town was buried in snowfall and the county was unable to clear it with its paltry snow removal equipment, McCoy sent his snow-cats down the mountain to open the roads. He was instrumental in starting the town's water district in the '50s and fire district in the '60s, sending his employees to build the infrastructure and man the equipment, much of which he also bought. McCoy later kept the town's fiscally unsteady hospital going for years with funding.

During the infamous winter of 1969, when an estimated 40 feet of snow dropped on Mammoth, visitors etched a sign in front of a thoroughly buried bus.

"He funneled money into it because he thought the community needed that hospital," says Bob Schotz, who operated the Woods Lodge at Lake George in the Lakes Basin for many years. "When it was about to fold up and close its doors, he kept it alive. And for years when I was on the school board, whenever anything was needed, he was right there."

McCoy rarely talked much about his contributions to the town, and never said anything about his frequent generosity toward individuals over the years. Schotz tells about a carpenter who worked full-time at Mammoth Mountain but became seriously ill. "He was sick for a year," says Schotz, "and every month, he got a check from McCoy. It wasn't insurance; it came out of his own pocket, because he felt that loyalty to an employee."

Now and then, immense snows buried Mammoth, but one of the most memorable of modern times was the snowfall of 1969. Stanford recalls that it started snowing on January 19 and didn't stop for six weeks. "We were snowed in until April 15. I figured that we had 240 percent of normal that year, a little over 40 feet," Stanford says, adding that the problem was compounded because the old-fashioned snowplows the county was using weren't up to the job. A string of cars parked

along Lake Mary Road were buried and eventually crushed by the snow, and when the snowplows finally were able to get in weeks later, they rolled over the vehicles and ripped the tops off of them. Meanwhile, Mammoth Mountain had to shut down when its chairlifts were completely buried, and snow drifted over the top of the expanded main ski lodge that by then stood three stories high.

As Mammoth Lakes grew in the 1960s, a new ethic of environmentalism began spreading that would have a sizable impact on the future of Mammoth Lakes and Mammoth Mountain. One of the most memorable battles was over a highway. The nearest road over the Sierra that could be traveled in winter lay just south of Lake Tahoe, but a plan to build one from Mammoth Lakes to the Central Valley near Fresno had been kicked around since the 1920s. Finally, in the early '70s, prodded by outside real estate and logging interests and some Forest Service officials who wanted to access new timber areas, the state began working on plans to build such a road using federal highway funds.

Above: A famous photo from the winter of '69 depicts snow drifting over the roof of the three-story Main Lodge. Below: In this view from the late 1960s, the gondola affords skiers a spectacular view of the Minarets.

Snow pillows like these on Mammoth Crest turn into natural terrain parks for athletes like Zack Yates.

Dubbed the Trans Sierra Highway, the road would cut through a vast, unbroken wilderness and, in the view of many alarmed Mammoth locals, transform their little mountain town into a suburb of Fresno. The proposed route would have started from Horseshoe Lake in the Lakes Basin and rolled past Reds Meadow and along the Granite Stairway in the Mammoth backcountry. Many of the area's leading citizens came out in fervent opposition to the road. Among them were the Eastern Sierra's horse packers—long-established, politically potent locals who were particularly horrified at the idea of a new highway slashing through the beloved backcountry where they earned their living. A determined group of Mammoth residents organized to fight the highway, and the Mono and Inyo county boards of supervisors finally weighed in against it. Although it would undoubtedly have boosted Dave McCoy's business by making Mammoth accessible to thousands of new skiers, many of his good friends were dead against the road, and he decided to remain neutral.

One of the packers who opposed the highway was Norman "Ike" Livermore, who owned the Mount Whitney Pack Station near Lone Pine. Livermore was more than locally influential; he was serving at the time as California's secretary of resources, under Governor Ronald Reagan. The packer was one of Reagan's trusted advisors, and he tried to impress upon the governor the irreversible harm the road would do and the ire it would raise among environmentalists and sportsmen. Nonetheless, the state began serious planning for the road at the beginning of the 1970s, surveying and marking its cuts and fills with stakes so that highway contractors could bid on the construction. No sooner had state workers finished their work than the normally law-abiding wives of prominent Mammoth Lakes businessmen sneaked out after dark and pulled up the stakes.

"The contractors who wanted to bid came in, but they couldn't find a lot of the stakes, for miles," says Woods Lodge operator Schotz, who resolutely fought the road. "There is some talk that people threw them away," Schotz innocently adds. The state had to restake the road, which delayed the project until the following year. In the meantime, Livermore continued to bend Reagan's ear about the drawbacks of the highway and the magnificent wilderness it would despoil. The packer was also able to extend his influence to Washington when he met President Richard Nixon's advisor John D. Ehrlichman at an environmental conference in Europe and discussed the impending Trans Sierra Highway with him.

Finally, in 1972, Governor Reagan came to Mammoth for a horse-packing trip through the very Sierra backcountry where the

To air is human: Skier Brad McFall launches into a bowl beneath Chair 22 on Lincoln Mountain.

road would pass. Reagan's party, led by Reds Meadow Pack Station owner Bob Tanner, numbered nearly a hundred, including assorted pols and a large press entourage. The Forest Service got word that Reagan was going to make an important announcement during the horse trip, and it also sent representatives to join the group.

The local Forest Service officials and others who had advocated the new project "felt that the road was a go, and they were delighted to see Reagan there to say so," says Schotz. Finally, when everyone was sitting around the campfire in Summit Meadow, Reagan told the assembly that he had an announcement to make. "He pulls out a little telegram from [President Nixon]," says Schotz. "It says that the President is withdrawing all funding for the construction of this road. [The contingent from the Forest Service that had favored the road] sat there like they had a wet fish thrown in their face."

Packer Bob Tanner explains that at the conference in Europe, Livermore had persuaded White House assistant Ehrlichman to get Nixon's signature on the document to block the road's funding. "It might have taken a lot of cocktails, but Ike got the job done," says Tanner. The highway was never built, preserving the Mammoth backcountry and, for better or worse, the Eastern Sierra's isolation. In 1984, Congress expanded the picturesque Minarets Wilderness behind Mammoth into a massive 228,500 acres bordering Yosemite National Park, including the land where the highway would have been built, and renamed it the Ansel Adams Wilderness, to the applause of environmentalists and most Eastern Sierrans.

While this was taking place on the east side of the Sierra, dramatic events were unfolding on the west side of the range that could have altered the history of Mammoth Mountain and

Above: Snow piled up beside the road to the ski area buries signs. Despite the heavy snowfall, the resort's plows keep the road open virtually all the time.

Mammoth Lakes just as thoroughly, although in a completely different way. In the book *Wild By Law*, Tom Turner told the remarkable story of Mineral King, which might have become one of the nation's top ski resorts, but where no resort was ever built. A few years after environmentalist David Brower conducted the survey for the Sierra Club and declared the majestic peaks and bowls above the U-shaped valley of Mineral King to be the ideal Sierra location for a ski area, the U.S. Forest Service decided to do something about it. In a story that closely parallels Mammoth Mountain's early ski-area history, the agency put out a prospectus for a ski area at Mineral King near Sequoia National Park in 1949. The prospectus called for "a hotel accommodating at least 100 people, a mile-long chairlift, a 2,100-foot T-bar lift and other features including 'over-the-snow' transportation from Three Rivers to the valley—a tracked vehicle of some sort," Turner reports. In response to its Mineral King prospectus, the Forest Service received not a single bid.

The glacially etched Mineral King valley was even more remote than Mammoth had been, many miles from any cleared road in winter, and it had no Dave McCoy already on hand operating rope tows. Still, Corty Hill, Mineral King's early champion, remained interested in seeing a resort built in the chain of mountains. The

Right: Dan Molnar surfs deep powder on the back side of Mammoth Mountain.

Above: The morning sun softens the snow for skiers as it lights the face of Mammoth Mountain.

railroad heir took a group including ski racer Andrea Mead Lawrence there in the early '50s to look it over. Hill also tried to persuade McCoy to leave Mammoth Mountain behind and develop a resort for him at Mineral King instead, but nothing could pry McCoy away from Mammoth.

"Corty would have bought everything I had here [at Mammoth] and have me go over there and do it for him. He asked me to do it. I said no," McCoy says.

Ski mountaineer and historian Wolfgang Lert adds, "There was a point at which, if Corty Hill had put in a small T-bar at Mineral King, he could have gotten the right to develop it. They could have built a Zermatt-type railroad down below. You could have taken the train up, and skied from some of the bowls around Mineral King back down to the train. It could have been a very interesting development—an American Zermatt."

In the end, however, things never came together to Hill's liking, and he never made a serious bid to build a resort there. Nothing progressed at Mineral King for almost a decade. However, Turner writes that in 1961, "a young geologist from Bakersfield

happened upon an intriguing rumor. Hiking in the basin over the Fourth of July weekend, he fell into conversation with a ranger who said he had heard that Walt Disney was planning a ski resort for the valley, with access to be provided by a monorail. Disney had quietly asked the Forest Service if it was still interested in entertaining development proposals for Mineral King."

The agency apparently approved, because Disney soon began buying property around the Mineral King area. In 1965, the Forest Service sent out a new prospectus for Mineral King, this time asking for bids of at least $3 million to build a ski resort with hotel facilities for at least 100 people, trams or chairlifts that could carry

Opposite: As Phil Dion performs a mute grab near Chair 14, the Minarets supply the incredible backdrop.

AIR MAMMOTH

Desert Airlines, Sierra Pacific, Royal West, Alpha Air—these were just some of the airlines that appeared over the years to fly Mammoth skiers up from Los Angeles. But regularly scheduled air service to Mammoth never really got off the ground, mainly because Mammoth's tiny airport couldn't accommodate large jets, and the small commuter airlines that tried to provide service lacked the dollars to make it work.

In 1957, Desert Airlines became the first to regularly transport skiers to the Eastern Sierra. It started running charters between Los Angeles and Bishop's little airport, where Mammoth Mountain buses picked up passengers and shuttled them to the ski area. In January of the following year, Desert began the first scheduled air service to the Eastern Sierra for Los Angeles skiers, carrying them from the old Lockheed Air Terminal in Burbank to Bishop. They flew 11 passengers at a time in small twin-engine DeHavilland Doves fitted with ski racks inside the cabin. The trip took about an hour and a half, not counting the extra hour tacked on for the bus ride to Mammoth.

In 1972, Dave McCoy got into the airline business himself. After he had loaned money to Sierra Pacific so that it could meet its payroll and the state was still threatening to shut it

Gary McCoy (left) had been working as a pilot for Sierra Pacific when his father (seated) tapped him to run the company.

down, Mammoth Mountain took it over. McCoy installed his son Gary, who had been working as a Sierra Pacific pilot, to lead the company. It flew 54-seat Convairs from L.A., Burbank, Fresno and Reno directly to Mammoth Lakes's airport until 1978, when Mammoth Mountain unloaded the airline after a few years of drought left the company in a belt-tightening phase. "There was another guy who wanted it real bad, and we weren't really airline people," Gary McCoy comments.

Wings West was next to transport skiers to Mammoth Lakes, but it soon departed to fly coastal routes that the company found more profitable. Royal West was another small airline that tried, but its British Aerospace planes "were just too big for what they were doing with them," Gary McCoy comments. "They couldn't get the business." A year later, Royal West shut down altogether. Then came Alpha Air, an airline operated by an Angeleno who was a Mammoth Lakes second-home owner. The company actually did well flying Cessnas and later 19-seat Beechcraft turboprops to Mammoth Lakes through the '80s and into the '90s. By the end of its run it was operating five scheduled flights a day from San Francisco, Los Angeles, Lake Tahoe and other cities into Mammoth. However, after it converted to Trans World Express, which

When Mammoth Mountain operated Sierra Pacific for several years in the 1970s, the airline flew skiers in from Los Angeles, Burbank, Fresno and Reno.

was affiliated with TWA, it became entangled in financial turmoil when the larger company filed for bankruptcy, and it finally shut down.

In the '90s, United Express gave it a try. However, United Airlines overbooked its flights so severely that it was constantly handing out hotel rooms and coupons to irate passengers whose ski vacations had been disrupted. "They were flying 19-seat Jetstreams, but they could only carry 11 people. They would overbook to 25 seats," recalls Bill Manning, manager of Mammoth Yosemite Airport. "You can imagine the consternation." The airline gave up its Mammoth operation after a few years.

The Mammoth airport south of town was originally just a dirt military airstrip built by the U.S. Army during World War II that couldn't even be used in winter until it was paved in 1959. The airport ownership changed several times, transferring to Mono County and the U.S. Forest Service before finally ending up in the hands of the town of Mammoth Lakes. Its various owners expanded and improved it over the years, but now the town, Mammoth Mountain and Intrawest are working on plans to give it a major upgrade so that it can land Boeing 757s. Those plans have been snagged by environmental opposition. For the time being, at least, skiers continue to travel to and from Mammoth the way they always have—driving their cars up and down the desert lanes of Highway 395. ❉

Mineral King might have become one of America's top ski resorts, and a major rival to Mammoth Mountain, but an epic environmental battle prevented its development.

2,000 people an hour, and parking facilities for more than 1,000 cars. With the resort looking larger than anything the Sierra Club had originally envisioned, the organization did an about-face and came out squarely against the project.

After the railroad and monorail ideas were abandoned, many of the practical questions about building the resort revolved around the road into Mineral King, which needed a $30 million upgrade. The state of California stepped in, saying that it would pay for the reconstruction of the road. By the summer of 1965, the Forest Service had received several bids for the ski resort, including one from Walt Disney. By the end of the year, Disney's bid had been accepted.

Disney's plan for the Mineral King ski resort far exceeded even what the Forest Service had called for in its revised prospectus. Disney proposed spending $35 million to build up to 27 chairlifts, along with "two hotels and a dormitory to accommodate 3,000 overnight guests plus a thousand employees, 10 restaurants and snack bars, a gas station, a theater, a chapel, a skating rink and [a 10-story underground garage] for 3,600 cars. All this, save the parking garage and service station, was designed to look like a village in the Swiss Alps. It would be six times as big as Squaw Valley," Turner writes. During the summers, it would offer visitors tennis, golf, fishing, horseback riding, swimming, hiking and camping. In October 1966, the Forest Service issued Disney a three-year planning permit for the development. Walt Disney died two months later, but his company carried on with the Mineral King plan.

In this classic shot, a telephoto lens makes Mount Ritter appear to tower over the top of Chair 1. Ritter actually stands about 10 miles distant.

If a ski resort that large and dazzlingly ornate had been built approximately three hours north of Los Angeles, it would unquestionably have drawn away much of Mammoth Mountain's Southern California customer base. It might have completely shut the tap of Southland skiers traveling up Highway 395. However, such an enormous proposal for such a remote wilderness touched off a monumental environmental battle with the Sierra Club. In 1968, the organization sued the Forest Service to stop the Disney project, supported by the National Park Service, which was less than enthusiastic about having such a major development next door to its park, especially since a part of the access road would have cut through Sequoia. The lawsuit wound through the courts for years, finally drawing in such Washington heavyweights as the Agriculture Secretary and two successive Interior secretaries, mostly on Disney's side.

In 1969, the Sierra Club managed to obtain an injunction against the resort project in U.S. District Court, which was overturned on appeal. The environmental group then asked the U.S. Supreme Court to review the appeal, which the Court agreed to do in 1971. The following year, in Sierra Club v. Morton, the High Court issued its decision. It upheld the appeal and dissolved the injunction, but it also left the door open for the Sierra Club to amend its original complaint, which the organization's lawyers soon did. This time, they asked that the Forest Service be ordered to prepare an Environmental Impact Statement for the project, according to a law that had passed in the interim.

By this time, the Mineral King controversy had fully captured the nation's attention. Disney, which had based part of its image on the popular nature films it produced, was getting tired of the fight and wary of the growing segment of the public that viewed the corporation as an environmental villain. In 1972, the state of California backed out of its decision to rebuild the road to Mineral King, sounding the death knell for the ski resort. By the time the Forest Service released its Environmental Impact Statement in 1975, the fight was essentially over. Three years later, Mineral King was officially added to Sequoia National Park, ending any possibility that a ski resort would be built there. ✪

David Schemenauer takes a direct route to the bottom of the mountain via Star Chute, one of Mammoth's toughest challenges.

From Hollywood to Mammoth

When the producers of the 2002 action-adventure film

The Scorpion King featuring WWF star The Rock were looking for

a place to shoot the movie's opening sequence, which takes place in an

ancient snow-covered wilderness, they picked June Lake, 15 miles north

of Mammoth. Aided by local contractors and suppliers, the film crew

spent months building a prehistoric-looking log structure and shooting

scenes in the parking lot of the June Mountain Ski Area.

A month later, another film crew was back in the Mammoth area to film daredevil stunt sequences over the Sierra for the extreme-sports spy film *XXX*, which stars Vin Diesel. For that movie, cinematographers flew over Convict Lake, southeast of Mammoth, and filmed adrenaline-pumping shots of snowboarders jumping out of airplanes and parachuting down to the snow.

Those crews were following an 80-year tradition of film-makers who trucked up from Hollywood to shoot Westerns and a mix of other movie genres in the big outdoors of the Eastern Sierra. Lying about 300 miles north of Hollywood, Mammoth has always held a special connection with the film capital. In the earliest days of Eastern Sierra skiing, McGee Mountain became a hangout for

Hollywood's elite. Corty Hill took over a hotel at Tom's Place near his relocated rope tow and remodeled it into a European-accented clubhouse-lodge for the Wooden Wings Ski Club, mostly a collection of Hollywood actors, directors and film technicians. In addition to Claudette Colbert, Hollywood royalty who traveled to McGee, Mammoth and Crestview in the '30s to ski—or try to learn—included Henry Fonda, Tyrone Power, Gary Cooper, Ginger Rogers, Robert Taylor, Barbara Stanwyck and Anthony Quinn.

In the days before jet travel was easy and common, many others came to the Eastern Sierra for location filming, or just to unwind. The rugged, photogenic rocks just west of Lone Pine called the Alabama Hills made that town the most popular spot in the region

For the 1939 action classic *Gunga Din*, set in the Himalayas, actors portraying turbaned ambushers hide in the Alabama Hills above others playing marching British soldiers.

for filming. One movie crew followed another there to shoot Westerns and other types of films. (See sidebar, page 160) When they needed to shoot snow-covered scenes or those with an alpine setting, they often continued up the highway to Mammoth. In the 1920s, Tex Cushion padded his income by loaning his dog teams to the film companies for silent movies with names like *Tundra* and *The Girl from Alaska*. He also helped make silent versions of *The Call of the Wild* and another Jack London tale, *White Fang*, although some of the films he worked on were never released. When the talkie 1935 version of *The Call of the Wild* was made, Clark Gable came to June Lake for the filming. Charlie Chaplin is said to have once dozed off *inside* the huge fireplace in the lobby of the vintage June Lake Lodge, built in 1928. Buster Keaton, Jimmy Durante, Ingrid Bergman and Samuel Goldwyn also slept at the lodge when

from the backcountry, the photo ran in the *Los Angeles Times*, and still adorns a wall in Dave McCoy's office beside other classic TJ photos. One of the photographer's favorites is a scenic shot of ski-lift chairs that he took while sitting atop the Chair 1 bullwheel.

"The chairs would swing out about 40 degrees, the wind was swirling and the sun was out, so it made an interesting photo," TJ says.

The irrepressible TJ, is known for his typical wardrobe of beachcomber-style jeans ending well above the ankle and red suspenders, which his friends naturally like to snap. He's a surfer, for 40 years a member of the San Onofre Surf Club in Southern California. He's also known as an inveterate ladies' man who always has a compliment for a female and a dry barb for his male cohorts, which they usually return. One Mammoth staffer and long-time friend comments, "TJ was famous for taking photographs of all of the most beautiful women on the mountain—ski school, ticket punchers, whomever it was—and always kept a complete file of promotional photographs of the best looking women in town. For company purposes, of course." ✪

TJ perched on the Chair 1 bullwheel to shoot this photo of windblown chairs, which he calls one of his favorites.

can be at the top of Mammoth Mountain and you have snow in June and views that look like the Himalayas? We've doubled for everything from Maine to the Rockies to the Alps to the Himalayas. Then you can go to a place like Bishop and double for Iowa, a Midwestern town, all just five hours away from Los Angeles. And where else are you going to find a ski resort like Mammoth Mountain Ski Area that has the shop, know-how and equipment to build you corrals that you can tow behind snowcats so you can haul up some Tibetan yaks?"

Although the movies are more exciting, TV commercials have always been the bread-and-butter for film coordinators in the Mammoth area. Dozens are filmed at Mammoth every year. "For every feature film, there's 15 commercials," Vanko says. "There's rarely a week that goes by where there isn't somebody shooting here. Car commercials in particular are here all the time. A lot of them need snow because they shoot their prototype cars in the spring for winter commercials. So you get a tremendous amount of production here just because we have snow on the ground in spring." Vanko says that NBC shot its promos for the Salt Lake City Winter Olympics at Mammoth, which doubled for Utah's mountains. Other products that have filmed TV ads around Mammoth include everything from MasterCard to Coors Light to Snickers candy bars. Before the 1980s, Roeser says that he assisted on TV ads for Ford, Budweiser and many others. He also worked on several shoots for print ads for Marlboro cigarettes, which favored the Mammoth area as a location for its cowboy scenes. Roeser appeared in some of the ads as a background Marlboro Man.

Many movie, TV and pop-music stars still vacation at Mammoth, although their visits are usually much more low-key than at glitzier resorts like Aspen. "We usually find out they've been here after they've left," says Mark Jobe, who works in Mammoth Mountain's marketing department. "We see them in some of the night spots around town." Among the eclectic range of celebrities spotted at Mammoth recently were actor Rob Lowe, *Friends* star Matt LeBlanc, alternative rockers the Red Hot Chili Peppers, rapper Coolio, some of the creators of *The Simpsons*, and action star Arnold Schwarzenegger. ✿

Right: As a storm clears over Mount Whitney, the rock formations of the Alabama Hills await their next film crew.

Previous page: The trout fishing in Long Valley south of Mammoth is considered among the best in the nation. Above: Hikers in the huge Ansel Adams Wilderness are rewarded with views like this reflection of Banner Peak in Thousand Island Lake.

Sierra Summer

One of the best-kept secrets of Mammoth locals is that they didn't

move to town because of the skiing, but for the weather-perfect summers.

Days are dependably sunny and hover mostly in the 80-degree range,

liquefying the mountain snow and opening up the immense,

wildflower-dotted backcountry. Mammoth's backyard is an enormous

complex of wilderness areas laced with hiking trails,

where no vehicles, including mountain bikes, are allowed.

The soaring stone walls and limpid alpine lakes of the 581,000-acre John Muir and 228,500-acre Ansel Adams wilderness areas lie just beyond the Mammoth Lakes Basin, which itself sits two minutes from the center of town. On the north and northeast, the town's hilly front yard is thickly forested with arrow-straight lodgepole pines.

Surrounded by all that glorious outdoors, Mammoth turns into an outdoor-sports mecca after the spring thaw. The trout fishing is some of America's best, and the rock climbing draws mountaineers from around the world. Hikers share the backcountry with the area's cluster of horse packers, whose predecessors were riding Sierra trails in the 1800s. The sport list expanded in the '80s, when the town became one of the original mountain-biking centers—and

again in the '90s, when two new golf courses were added. Most of the world might recognize Mammoth as a snow capital, but Southern Californians are clued in to Mammoth's summer draws. So are many San Francisco Bay Area and Central Valley residents, who can reach the Eastern Sierra by driving through Yosemite starting in late spring. While around a million visitors came to Mammoth in winter over the past few years, summer visitors have been averaging around a million and a half.

A few pastimes that haven't changed much in the past century played major roles in defining the culture of the region. The Eastern Sierra has been sold to tourists as a trout-fishing paradise since the dawn of the 1900s, and fishing tourism has been a critical part of the local economy. Pictures of trout grace the logos of shops and

Shimmering waters and a chance for rainbow trout—it's a summer day on Twin Lakes.

civic organizations, and one of the most anxiously awaited annual events is the opening of fishing season. That weekend, thousands of anglers from Southern California jam into Bishop and Mammoth before dispersing to mountain lakes and streams that have just been unlocked from blankets of snow and ice. Fishing at Crowley Lake has become a traditional opening-day rite; more anglers collect there than at any other single spot. Crowley is the largest fish-bearing lake in the Eastern Sierra, lying directly alongside Highway 395 on the drive to Mammoth, and is known for its fat, pink-fleshed trout. In years past, fishermen stood shoulder to shoulder casting from the lakeshore that opening weekend, and most locals waited a week until the bedlam died down before they ventured there to fish. Uncooperative weather kept the opening-day numbers down in recent years, but anglers still streamed in later in the season.

The stories about giant trout leaping out of the Owens River and snatching mule deer off the banks aren't true, but the walls of a Bishop cafe really are adorned with locally-caught and mounted trophy trout in the 25-pound range. California state records for brown

(26 pounds eight ounces) and brook trout (nine pounds 12 ounces) came from Mono County waters. And when Fred Rowe talks about catching and releasing a hundred fish a day on the San Joaquin River, a top fly-fishing spot, that story is true, too. Rowe is a part-time fishing guide who spends most days working as a checker in a Bishop supermarket. He has been fishing the Eastern Sierra since he started coming on vacations in the 1970s when he was 15. Rowe likes to head for the San Joaquin near Mammoth to fish for the grand slam of trout—rainbow, brown, brook and golden—or to the celebrated wild-trout fishery at volcanically warmed Hot Creek. He explains that Mammoth lies at the epicenter of a fishing heaven.

Opposite: Silver Lake is part of the June Lake chain, which is known for its monster trout.

A summer day on Lake Mary, one of many gemlike waters in the Mammoth Lakes Basin.

"You have all the fishing that's right there at Mammoth proper, plus Crowley Lake on the south, the June Lake Loop on the north, and the San Joaquin on the West." he notes. "If you add the fishing around Bishop and Bridgeport, that opens up the entire Eastern Sierra that's within an hour of Mammoth."

Throughout the spring and summer, aerospace workers on their days off, university students, retired businessmen and young families ride up to Mammoth to go trout fishing. Besides heading to Crowley, they might end up casting from the shores of the snaking

Opposite: Tobacco Creek cascades over the rocks beneath the granite walls of the Sierra.

Owens River, from a boat on Lake Mary beneath cone-shaped Crystal Crag, or if they're more ambitious, hiking up to backcountry lakes over Duck Pass. Serious trophy fishermen often head for some of the lakes that have produced the most monster trout over the past decade, Twin Lakes near Bridgeport, a second pair of waters named Twin Lakes in the Mammoth Lakes Basin, or the June Lake chain. Despite those big catches, some old-timers groused in the '80s and '90s that after years of heavy fish stocking and angling, the average trout coming out of the Eastern Sierra waters weren't nearly the size that they once were. One Eastern Sierran decided to do something about that. Tim Alpers, a former Mono County supervisor, started raising oversized trout on his ranch between Mammoth and June and stocking them in local waters, with state approval.

"From going fishing with his dad when he was a young child, Tim has a vision in his mind of what the perfect trout looks like,"

MAMMOTH'S BEAR MAN

Mammoth Lakes is bear country. A large population of black bears inhabits the national forest that sprawls for miles around the town, and over the past decade they started lumbering more often down Mammoth's streets. They climb into trash bins, break into cars and get into other trouble looking for an easy meal. In most places around the country, bears that are fed by tourists or crash into cars or homes to get food usually end up being shot as public nuisances. As the saying goes, "a fed bear is a dead bear." That's where Steve Searles comes in. Searles, a longtime Mammoth hunter and trapper, has contracted with the town of Mammoth Lakes to discourage bears from hanging around buildings and yards in town, using his own nonlethal approach for putting the fear of man back into the animals.

He hassles bears with a variety of flashing and noise-making devices and other gear, and the program has been very successful. Since the town first enlisted Searles' services in the '90s, not a single nuisance bear has been killed.

"We use nonlethal techniques to coexist with the wildlife: flash-bang devices, pyrotechnics, rubber bullets, rubber buckshot," Searles explains. Mammoth's black bears have not exact-

Steve Searles devised a non-lethal program for dealing with interloping bears that has been celebrated in the media and adopted by other local governments.

ly been shrinking violets over the years. They occasionally enter houses, like one bear that shuffled through the front door of a Mammoth home and headed straight for the refrigerator, snacking on its contents while the shaken residents fled upstairs to call police. In another incident years ago, a bear crashed into the town's Baskin-Robbins shop at night and devoured most of its ice cream.

But after the bears are treated rudely by Searles, they steer clear of humans. Several bears had actually taken up residence in crawl spaces and foundations under buildings in the middle of Mammoth Lakes in the '90s, but after Searles started harassing them, they began running whenever they saw his truck pull up.

"The old way used to be to go shoot the bear, and that worked fine." Searles says. "Today people aren't interested in eating the bear or wearing it as a jacket. They like their wildlife on the hoof and enjoy it alive rather than dead."

Through his bear work, the bearded, ursine Searles has become a celebrity. Stories about him have appeared in the *Los Angeles Times*, *San Francisco Chronicle*, *Seattle Times* and *Baltimore Sun*, and he has been featured on the *Today Show*, and *NBC News*, *ABC News*, CNN and Fox, and on Canadian and

German TV. His approach to dealing with bears has now been adopted at Whistler in British Columbia and in Yosemite, and he has been hired to speak to police about dealing with bear problems in New Jersey, Maryland and Tennessee. Searles appreciates the interest, and the opportunity Mammoth Lakes gave him to develop his approach. Once bears started routinely crossing paths with people in town, Searles says, "our community took the easy way out and chose to teach the smarter of the two animals—the bears." ❂

Bears get into trouble when they come into Mammoth and root through trash bins or other places to find meals.

Ranchers round up cattle at sunrise in McGee Canyon, not far from Mammoth Lakes.

Rowe says of Alpers. "You can almost instantly tell when someone's describing an Alpers rainbow. The prettiest rainbow you could ever see, upwards of 10, 12 pounds, that's what he's stocking."

One of the early fishing experts in Independence was none other than Dave McCoy, who never seems far from any Eastern Sierra history that has anything to do with the outdoors. Somehow, at age 19, McCoy attracted a front-page article in the *Inyo Independent* on July 20, 1934, one of the first times he ever passed

Opposite: Before his time was occupied with running Mammoth Mountain, Dave McCoy worked as a hunting and flyfishing guide and occasionally posed for print advertisements with outdoorsy themes.

through the Eastern Sierra. "Makes Own Way by Tying Flies," the headline read, and the article that followed noted that he had tied thousands of royal coachmen, black gnats and hackles in his spare time, and before heading back up to Washington, he was offering to sell them to fishermen. "He believes the secret of successful fly fishing is in using small hooks with a six- to nine-foot leader. Of course, one should know how to cast," the newspaper pointed out helpfully.

After fishing, the two activities that lure more people to Mammoth in summer than any other sports are backpacking and day hiking. Countless hiking routes climb from nearby trailheads into the cool Sierra backcountry, where trekkers amble through dense fir and pine forests, passing yellow-bellied marmots sunning themselves on slabs of granite and Clark's nutcrackers crying shrilly overhead. The 211-mile John Muir Trail, which overlaps with the 2,650-mile interstate Pacific Crest Trail, slices directly through the

In a scene that has been replayed in the Eastern Sierra for more than a century, a lone horse packer leads his string past Thousand Island Lake.

Devils Postpile National Monument and Agnew Meadows west of Mammoth Mountain. Hardier backpackers take the John Muir through the emerald Mammoth backcountry for as long as they care to hike, on their way to camp, fish backcountry lakes or climb rock faces. Some longer treks over the Sierra Crest continue into remote reaches of Yosemite National Park. Those with less time or inclination to cover a lot of ground take shorter backcountry hikes and return to soak in a hot tub by evening.

The Eastern Sierra has been a horse-packing capital for so long that the biggest celebration in the nearby town of Bishop each spring is Mule Days, which features mule parades, mule-shoeing contests and mule races. It draws tens of thousands of Southern Californians into the town of only 3,700 residents. For many decades the Eastern Sierra horse packers have been pillars of the community, highly respected rugged indi-

Gus Weber built many pack trails in the Eastern Sierra and was Mammoth Mountain's first ski school director.

vidualists. Their political influence grew over the years, and some were elected county supervisors or served in other leadership roles. Some of the pack outfits are family businesses, handed down from generation to generation. Former Inyo County Supervisor Herb London is passing the reins of the Rock Creek Pack Station to his son Craig, and Bob Tanner's son Bobby helps run the Reds Meadow Pack Station. Sometimes they're traded back and forth between packing families. Charlie Summers, one of the town founders, started the Mammoth Lakes Pack Outfit with his son Lloyd out of the log hotel he built in the

Opposite: Wild mule ears bloom on a hillside in front of Mammoth Mountain, still covered with patches of summer snow.

Packer Lou Roeser directs a pack string through Cascade Meadows. He bought the Mammoth Lakes Pack Outfit from Lee Summers, ran it for four decades and then sold it back to Lee's son, John.

Old Mammoth meadow in 1918. Four decades later, Charlie's grandson Lee sold the pack station to Lou Roeser, who ran it for four decades with his family before he retired and sold it back to Lee's son John a few years ago. Meanwhile, Roeser's own son Lee now runs the McGee Creek Pack Station with his wife Jennifer.

The packers are still regarded as romantic, colorful figures and have plenty of political clout, but these days they always seem to be raising someone's ire. In response, some of them complain that they are being hounded out of business by hikers, environmentalists and the Forest Service. Backpackers and horse packers both travel up many of the very same trails through the Sierra's magnificent wilderness, and the hikers have complained that while they were held to quotas on trails, horse packers get unfair priority to the lands. Meanwhile, environmentalists have complained about the practices of a few packers, such as cutting down trees on their routes. Even the horse packers' introduction of trout into numerous fishless backcountry lakes a century ago, long hailed as a fine public service, has been called into question. A local scientist discovered in the '90s that the non-native fish were devouring a native species, the mountain yellow-legged frog, to the point that it was nearly extinct. The irony

Left: From left to right, Mount Morrison, Laurel Mountain and Bloody Mountain rise above the volcanically active upper Long Valley.

In the 1980s, Mammoth was one of the first places to become a mountain bike mecca.

is that the packers who are now under fire from some environmentalists and wilderness purists for many years were the front-line Sierra environmentalists, protecting the backcountry from a multitude of incursions. Times changed, and so did the ways that the wilderness is used, but for the most part the packers didn't. Beyond local politics, however, their horseback trips remain highly popular with the wider public.

The packers travel routes up different backcountry drainages, setting out directly from Mammoth or from Reds Meadow to the west and Convict Lake, Rock Creek and McGee Creek south of town. Several others ride Inyo County trails. They carry passengers on horse and mule caravans through the John Muir and Ansel Adams wilderness areas, some on trips with themes like photography, fly fishing or searching for wild mustangs. Packers also offer horse drives, where guests help transport the packers' stock by driving the animals through the high desert to winter pastures in the Owens Valley or back up to the high country.

Mountain bikes weren't invented in Mammoth, but it was one of the first places where people carted them out to see what they could do. Rolling over the Mammoth landscape on fat-tire bikes remains one of the town's most popular sports. Bike trails have been carved through the pine forests on the federal lands that encircle the town, and those tracks connect with dirt back roads to open up hundreds of square miles of public land to biking. One network splays through the Knolls at the northeastern base of Mammoth Mountain, another curls through the Lakes Basin where one mountain-bike trail encircles Horseshoe Lake.

Mountain bikers can ride trails and back roads all the way from Mammoth to June Lake, or pedal to many of the area's eccentric geologic formations. A single-track lane runs from the Knolls to the Inyo Craters, a pair of wide, deep volcanic depressions inlaid with jade-colored ponds a few miles from town. North of June, the East Craters Loop runs around the moonscape at the Mono Craters, a chain of tall, steep-sided obsidian domes. A favorite summer ride is the 1,500-foot plunge down the paved road—closed to traffic except shuttle buses—from Minaret Summit near the Mammoth Main Lodge to the magnificent backcountry of Reds Meadow. Riders sometimes grind to a stop at the entrance to the weirdly shaped Devils

Above: Mammoth Mountain has remained a racing venue during the summer, frequently hosting the National Off Road Bike Association Championships. Below: A pro rider wheels his bike through a dual slalom race at Mammoth.

Postpile, the lush meadows surrounding Sotcher Lake, or the Middle Fork of the San Joaquin.

Given Dave McCoy's inclination to go bushwhacking through steep scrubland on his mountain bike after his 86th birthday, it shouldn't be surprising that his resort wheeled wholeheartedly into the sport. In the summertime, Mammoth Mountain Ski Area is transformed into the Mammoth Mountain Bike Park, lined with 80 miles of single-track dirt trails. In a parallel to the skiing layout, some are more advanced tracks that drop from the mountain summit, while others wind more easily through the pines and open slopes below. Still open is the famous Kamikaze, a steep thrill ride that dives down the west side of Mammoth Mountain, one of its original fat-tire trails.

"The Kamikaze is more of an experience than an enjoyable ride through the trees like the other trails are," says Dave Geirman, Mammoth Mountain's bike park manager. "It's kind of like bungee jumping—you want to say you've done it."

Less frantic trails are more abundant, like Downtown, which meanders down the east side of the mountain to end up at the new North Village.

The bike park's designers—McCoy, Geirman and another mountain manager, Bill Cockroft—had to rethink their original plan of using the ski area's service roads for bike trails. ("They were way too rocky and steep," Geirman says.) Instead, they cut special mountain-bike trails, adding a few new ones every year. Sticking with its dedication to racing, Mammoth Mountain has frequently hosted the National Off Road Bike Association (NORBA) races, which include cross-country, downhill, uphill and dual-slalom competitions.

"Downhilling is a radical sport," Geirman says. "For the NORBA race, we've designed and built two world-class, extremely technical high-speed downhills. The Kamikaze was all about speed, but the new courses are about speed and also maneuvering over rocks and down jumps."

Lately, the resort has been trying to attract more extreme hard-core bikers by building X Zones—technical courses that nose-dive even more precipitously and are also broken up with challenges like jumps, berms and logs.

Rock climbing isn't exactly new to the Eastern Sierra. In his 1872 book *Mountaineering in the Sierra Nevada*, geologist Clarence King describes the Sierra around Mammoth Mountain and gives a detailed account of his "first ascent" of the summit of Mount Whitney. Later, an embarrassed King had to acknowledge that he had actually climbed the wrong mountain by mistake. In the meantime, a few Lone Pine fishermen on a day's outing to escape the valley heat climbed to the real Whitney summit, and a few other parties followed them to the top. King had to settle later for an unexceptional follow-up ascent.

Bishop began growing into a climbing center many decades ago. Among the mountaineers who made the Owens Valley their home for a few years, or a few decades, were some celebrated names: the irrepressible Norman Clyde, Doug Robinson, John Fischer and Galen Rowell. By the 1970s, a sizable community of rock climbers had settled in Bishop to do traditional base-to-summit mountaineering on the order of King's, or to clamber up the big boulders near Bishop. Some mountaineers traveled to the Eastern Sierra from Yosemite after climbing its famous big walls, El Capitan and Half Dome, which lie only a few hours from Mammoth in summer. They ascended peaks in the 12,000- to 13,000-foot range, including the Minarets and Mount Ritter near Mammoth.

Right: The big rocks just outside of Bishop draw bouldering aficionados from around the world.

Now climbers are moving to Mammoth for the area's newly emerging variation, sport climbing, making the town a component in a wider climbing mecca. Rather than ascending the cracks, chimneys and other natural rock features in the manner of traditional climbers, sport climbers spend their days muscling themselves up a variety of short roped routes on blank walls and cliff faces. The sport opened up miles of new Sierra terrain that wasn't considered climbable before. The volcanic tuff in the Owens River Gorge below Crowley Lake has emerged as one of the most popular sport-climbing draws, along with the sheer headwall behind the Lakes Basin named the Mammoth Crest and the volcanic-rock faces near the headwaters of the Owens River.

Climbers still travel to Bishop just to climb the big boulders scattered in pockets around the Buttermilk, the most famous bouldering area just west of the town. And no one seems to know how the Happy Boulders and the Sad Boulders north of Bishop got their names, but the monikers have nothing to do with their rankings by climbers. Both are favorite hangouts.

Allan Pietrasanta is a sporty, bearded former rock-climbing guide who started a sports-gear and computer-case company in Bishop while he watched Eastern Sierra rock climbing evolve over the past few decades.

"High-level bouldering with no ropes at all has grown in the last decade," Pietrasanta says. "People are doing really hard stuff, 20, 30 feet off the ground. It's phenomenal. There are people that come to Bishop that never uncoil a rope. They could climb here for three weeks, just bouldering."

"The Eastern Sierra has terrain for all three kinds of climbing—big peaks, countless small cliffs and infinite boulders," he continues. "Mammoth and Bishop have reached a synergy, because Mammoth offers world-class sport climbing while Bishop offers world-class bouldering. There's a way bigger climbing population living in Mammoth than there was 20 years ago because it's such a desirable place, combined with the climbing around Bishop that has also exploded. In a spring or fall weekend, there will be hundreds of climbers from a dozen countries in Inyo and Mono counties."

Mammoth golfers can now tee off on their choice of courses, one a nine-hole and the other an 18-hole. The town also features a top-notch motocross track, probably for no other reason than that Dave McCoy loved the sport. In 1968 he and one of his ski area managers, Don Rake, decided to hold a motocross competition at Mammoth. They built the track, and the Mammoth Motocross has been run every summer since. McCoy donated the equipment, fencing, water trucks and graders and installed a sprinkler system in the early days. He also competed himself, winning many of the Old Timers' races over the years. On his 86th birthday, his employees gave him a brand new state-of-the-art motocross bike, which he took out for the occasional spin, to the dismay of his wife, Roma.

Mammoth's culture may have been largely shaped around outdoor sports, but it does have its other facets. Summer is the time when the town holds music festivals, some of them presented in the semi-outdoors in big-top tents pitched in different spots around Mammoth. The oldest is the Sierra Summer Festival, which once

In recent years the Owens River Gorge between Bishop and Mammoth Lakes has become a favorite locale for sport climbers.

featured major rock and country acts but has since morphed into a series of classical chamber music and orchestra concerts. Each July, strains of Mozart, Brahms or Tchaikovsky bounce off of Mammoth Mountain when the Eastern Sierra Symphony Orchestra performs at the Main Lodge. The group, formed in 1983 and made up partly of amateur local musicians, is led by the conductor of the Beverly Hills Symphony Orchestra, Bogidar Avramov. Another event, the Mammoth Lakes Jazz Jubilee, draws a lineup of groups playing Dixieland, swing and other jazz. Meanwhile, locals say that they find the Mammoth Festival of Beers and Bluesapalooza the most intoxicating. Its name describes the event pretty well. Microbreweries from around California and beyond present their products, and the Festival of Beers Grand Tasting, which offers unlimited beer sampling, caps the event. Meanwhile, blues bands hammer out electric and acoustic sets, and the festival turns into a big, freewheeling party. Rounding out the summertime

Above: The Sierra Star Golf Course, added in the '90s, provided Mammoth Lakes with its first 18-hole course. Below: Hikers can wander through the enormous Mammoth backcountry for an afternoon, or go trekking for weeks.

SKY PILOT

Some outdoorsy locals and visitors have their own unusual perspective of the Mammoth backcountry—they view it from thousands of feet up as they soar over it in hang gliders. Few in the world are better at it than Kari Castle. The Owens Valley resident has won the women's hang gliding world championship three times, including in summer of 2002, and has been the women's national champion for the past 13 years. Castle has set world records, including the women's distance mark with a spectacular 250-mile flight, and in 2001 she became the first woman to make the U.S. national team. Currently ranked sixth overall in the country, the dynamic Castle works as a hang gliding guide from her Bishop home when she isn't traveling around the globe to competitions. If that schedule isn't busy enough, she has also won the women's national paragliding championships twice.

The Owens Valley retains a mystique for hang glider pilots, because many of the early distance records were set from starts above Lone Pine and other nearby spots. The scorching summer heat in the deep valley beneath the sheer Eastern Sierra cliffs create thermals that provide ultrastrong lift—"big air," as hang glider pilots call it. "When you fly here, it's some of the most extreme air you can find in the world," Castle comments. "It's some of the biggest air I've ever had, and I've traveled a lot in the world. You can fly 100 miles really easy here, and people just love that." Today, improvements in equipment and launching techniques have allowed pilots to set longer distance records in flatter places (the latest hot spot is Zapata, Texas, where Castle set her distance mark), but flyers still flock to the legendary Owens Valley from all over the world. Some of her recent hang gliding clients have hailed from Japan, England, Australia, Brazil and the Caribbean.

Castle, who has flown as high as 23,000 feet, says that she sometimes takes her clients for less brutal rides off of McGee Mountain or the mountains above Lee Vining in Mono County, and she loves to launch off of the Mammoth Mountain summit. "Mammoth Mountain is one of my favorite places to fly off; it's so absolutely beautiful there," she says. "It's susceptible to wind, but on the days that it's not windy and is flyable, it's magic to be looking over the Minarets and back at the lakes. We've flown pretty deep into the Sierra to the south

Owens Valley resident Kari Castle, who has set a women's distance record of 250 miles, travels the globe to compete in hang-gliding contests.

and then come out by McGee." She flies Mammoth summer and winter, carrying her hang glider to the summit in the gondola by arrangement with the ski area.

The 41-year-old pilot likes to ski and snowboard on Mammoth Mountain too, although she usually spends most of the California winter months in Australia. When she's at home in the Owens Valley in summer, she prefers to go climbing in the Owens River Gorge and bouldering in the Buttermilk, and also mountain biking and backpacking. Still, she says, her favorite way of traveling through the Eastern Sierra backcountry is by air. "It's much easier than hiking," she laughs. ✺

Castle won her third women's hang gliding world championship in 2002 at Chelan Butte, Washington, and has been the national women's champion for more than a decade.

A rainbow graces the wooly mammoth sculpture that stands outside of the Mammoth Mountain Inn.

fare, a couple of weekend arts festivals give Mammoth painters, photographers and other artists and craftsmen a chance to sell their works from outdoor booths.

One more pair of summer sports brings outdoorsy people to Mammoth: skiing and snowboarding. Mammoth's famous late season often stretches into the month of June. Some years when the snow has piled high enough and the weather stays reasonably cool, the ski area has remained open in August. More than a few Mammoth skiers have stories to tell about carving turns through a light July snowstorm. Years ago, Mammoth Mountain used to allow anyone who skied on Christmas Day to use that same lift ticket for a free day of skiing in May or later. Some locals would merrily drive up to the Main Lodge parking lot in the late Yule afternoon and pick discarded lift tickets up off the ground, then use them to ski all spring and summer. Some say it's their favorite time of year. The crowds are gone, the corn snow is fine, and they can ski or snow-board through the mild, sun-drenched days in their T-shirts. ☼

Right: A descending sun sets ablaze a spreading cloud formation above the Sierra.

Previous page: When summer comes to Little Lakes Valley at Rock Creek Canyon, the color palette expands dramatically. Above: With Mammoth Mountain as a backdrop, skier Chris Samuels wheels over the backcountry.

chapter 9

Seasons of Change

Anyone who has vacationed at Mammoth for years but hasn't

visited the town lately might be amazed at the way it has changed.

The quirky mountain town that sprouted and grew spontaneously with

little in the way of real planning is being thoroughly revamped.

The most conspicuous addition is the new Village at Mammoth

(originally known as North Village) at the foot of Mammoth Mountain,

designed to provide 3,000 condo and hotel rooms and 150,000

square feet of space for retail shops and restaurants.

Included are 25,000 square feet of new Mammoth Mountain base facilities, with a 15-passenger gondola to transport skiers directly up to the slopes and back down again. The Village at Mammoth provides Mammoth Lakes with the center it never had, a place for pedestrians in a community that used to be so completely car-oriented that it never bothered to build sidewalks until the late '90s.

This newest phase of building began in the '90s with the construction of a string of other condominiums and an 18-hole golf course. Some longtime locals look sadly at the way the town

is being transformed into a tony resort, while other residents, particularly Mammoth's business community, are overjoyed at what they see as a town finally living up to its potential.

Most of this change is being wrought by Intrawest Corp.— one of the largest real estate developers in the ski business— together with Mammoth Mountain. Intrawest bought 59 percent of the ski area in the late '90s, but the deal was structured so that Dave McCoy retained control of the ski operation, while Intrawest is fully in charge of the in-town real estate development.

Intrawest bought in following the most tumultuous years in

Chair 23, added in the early 1980s, gave skiers a new way to climb to the summit.

Mammoth Mountain's history, from the mid '80s to the late '90s. The resort had continued to grow, and by 1985 McCoy had 31 ski lifts climbing its 3,500 skiable acres. Until then, the resort's skier numbers had never really faltered, rising steadily from the time McCoy had installed Chair 1. There had always been exceptions, of course, like those odd, occasional periods when Mammoth's snow levels dipped below normal and its skier numbers slipped correspondingly. But McCoy, who turned 70 in 1985, continued to operate his ski resort in his maverick, independent way, keeping faith in his mountain's natural assets and its magnetic effect on skiers. While most ski areas had by then installed at least rudimentary snowmaking equipment, it didn't seem necessary at Mammoth Mountain, which had rarely suffered a prolonged drought.

McCoy had also always relied on the "build it and they will come" approach, and didn't believe in massive Southern California marketing campaigns. After Mammoth Mountain hit an all-time high of more than 1.4 million skier visits in 1985-86 following three decades of steady growth, who could argue? Not the *Wall Street Journal*, which praised McCoy's management style and entrepreneurial spirit in a front-page feature entitled "Heights of Success." Nor the *Los Angeles Times*, which lauded McCoy in a 1986 feature headlined, "Man Meets Mountain: A Mammoth Success Story," naming him "monarch of the busiest ski area in the United States." The media zeroed in on McCoy in the mid 1980s not only because of Mammoth's position at the industry's summit, but also because by that time all of the nation's other top ski resorts had been taken over by massive corporations like Apex Oil and Ralston Purina. In a 1986 article in *Sports Illustrated*, William Oscar Johnson noted that McCoy was "sadly, the last of his particular

In the late '90s, as equipment made off-piste adventures easier, more skiers and snowboarders explored the Mammoth backcountry. Skier: Todd Miller in Rock Chute.

breed of mountain man, the last to run his whole multimillion dollar shebang by himself."

With Mammoth Mountain soaring, McCoy decided to chase one of his long-standing dreams. In the summer of 1986, he purchased June Mountain, which had been started by a Southern Californian named Bud Hayward in the early 1960s. June had always been an undercapitalized, second-class resort that finally edged near bankruptcy in the mid '80s. Mammoth's owner had a handshake deal with Hayward that if he was ever ready to part with June, he would let McCoy know. "That's exactly what happened," McCoy told a reporter after the acquisition. "I made him a deal he couldn't turn down."

McCoy also began to turn his operation over to his children, giving each of them 10 percent of his company as gifts and naming son Gary general manager of Mammoth Mountain while installing daughter Kandi in the same position at June.

June Mountain rises above a perfectly gorgeous, horseshoe-shaped canyon just beyond the border of Yosemite National Park, speckled with a chain of sapphire lakes. Most of its ski terrain is gentle, a perfect resort for beginners and intermediates, but its lifts were out of date and its on-mountain facilities needed refurbishing. McCoy borrowed heavily for the capital to buy June Mountain, then immediately set to work upgrading it with high-speed detachable quad lifts and a new high-tech tram. However, McCoy had much more in mind than that for June, which sits about 20 miles by car from Mammoth Mountain, but only about six crow miles. He had long envisioned transforming the Sierra between Mammoth and June into a grand Alps-style skiing network by linking the two resorts with a system of ski lifts.

"Probably 12 or 15 lifts would be needed to connect Mammoth and June, at a minimum," McCoy told the *Los Angeles*

Lots of skiers riding Chair 23 consider jumping into Drop Out Chutes. Not many do it. Skier: Nathan Wallace,

Times. "You could do it like a sawtooth, going up and down. [Or] you could actually connect them with one transportation system," he said, and develop some of the best canyons or ridges along the way. Either way, it would create an immense, multimountain skiing complex that Mammoth's owner estimated would be "comparable to European ski areas where as many as 250,000 skiers are accommodated in a day."

However, that was when Dave McCoy's usual good luck suddenly abandoned him. The first season after the June Mountain purchase, when his company was heavily laden with debt, the snow didn't fall in Mammoth. With no snowmaking machinery for backup, the ski area was unable to open until late in the season. Mammoth Mountain's skier visits dropped abruptly, plunging in one year from over 1.4 million to around 700,000.

"We had a catastrophically bad year that year," Mammoth Mountain CEO Rusty Gregory says, recalling that during that winter "there was a picture in the *L.A. Times* of someone riding a mountain bike at the bottom of Chair 2." The season turned out to be the beginning of an extended drought that plagued Mammoth off and on for the next decade. Every normal or near-normal season was followed by a year or two of very little snow.

Skiers always go where the snow is, but by the early '90s they were beginning to bypass Mammoth for other reasons. Skiing had swiftly gone upmarket. Resorts like Vail and Deer Valley were attracting baby boomers by pampering them with deluxe trappings such as lavish lodges, chic restaurants and valets to carry their skis for them. It was most unlike Mammoth, which had always offered an unadorned, no-frills experience everywhere except on the slopes, where McCoy felt it counted.

"We kept playing the same tune," says John Armstrong, "but musical tastes had changed."

With his resort in a serious downturn, McCoy was forced to put off his ambitious plans to create a Mammoth-to-June megaresort and concentrate instead on bringing his ski area back.

The town of Mammoth Lakes, with its economy closely tied to Mammoth Mountain's, naturally suffered during the drought years. But it had already been in an economic tailspin before that. A severe recession in Southern California had depressed tourism in the entire Eastern Sierra, hurting the town's businesses throughout the year. Also, after a series of major earthquakes rattled the Eastern Sierra in the early '80s, word began circulating about a possible volcanic eruption in the Long Valley Caldera, and real estate values in the town sagged. National media occasionally came to town to do stories about the volcanic stirrings, often portraying it as an imminent catastrophe. Some less respectable tabloid TV

Above the 'pipe. Skier: Shannon Schad. Below: Dave McCoy bought June Mountain in 1986 and immediately began upgrading its facilities to take advantage of its gentle terrain.

Creating a white wave in Drop Out Chutes. Skier: Silver Chesak.

shows even dramatized the caldera story by playing attention-grabbing video of an erupting Mount St. Helens, giving some viewers the mistaken impression that Mammoth Mountain had already exploded. Since Highway 203 was then the only road in and out of Mammoth, a second road out to U.S. 395 was hastily added as an earthquake escape route.

Mammoth Lakes was incorporated as a town in 1984, partly because it didn't like the way the county was handling its tourism marketing. Another reason was the townsfolk's feeling that they were being shortchanged on services, especially since Mammoth Lakes had become by far Mono County's largest population center.

"They had parks all over the county, and our kids were playing in rock fields," says Kirk Stapp, who has served on the town council since it was first formed. The town set up government offices, a police force and a new marketing bureau, but problems persisted. From the combined effects of the loss of skiers, the recession and the volcano scare, many businesses in Mammoth were forced to close their doors. Some years, the town was practically deserted outside of the peak

Left: In the '80s, McCoy developed still-unfulfilled plans to link Mammoth Mountain with June Mountain, which would have created a vast skiing complex.

STEVE KLASSEN:
CLIFF RIDER

Riders have to be strong, agile and quick-witted to survive in the world of extreme snowboarding. Steve Klassen is all three, and that's why he's one of the top names in the sport. Klassen, who lives in Mammoth Lakes, has won the intense King of the Hill competition in Valdez, Alaska, twice, and the cliffhanging Red Bull Extreme in Verbier, Switzerland, three times. He also took the big-mountain event in the 2000 NBC Gravity Games.

Extreme snowboarding competitions, usually held on the most electrifyingly steep mountainsides their organizers can find, are judged on the basis of speed, fluidity, control, amount of air and difficulty of the snowboarder's line. Klassen is known for his well-dialed lines and fast, fluid rides, but says that he learned an important lesson in one of his early competitions when he missed his route down a sheer mountainside of jagged rock.

"I thought I went into a certain chute, but I didn't spot my entrance like I should have and it was actually one chute over to the side," he says. "There was a way through, but it was the scariest move I've ever made in my life. It was probably more than 150 feet of vertical rock, and I had to hop and make it

Klassen, victor in two King of the Hill competitions and three Red Bull Extremes, takes a break in his Mammoth Lakes snowboarding shop.

down this little shelf. I did it, but I really don't make mistakes like that anymore."

Klassen was a three-time All-American at the University of Southern California, which he attended on a pole-vaulting scholarship, and made the Olympic trials in the sport but couldn't compete because of a pulled hamstring. He grew up in Boulder and lived for a while in Vail, but moved to Mammoth in 1989 because the mountain's precipitous, open, rocky terrain better suited his style. "It's a way better mountain for steeps, and that's what I've always been drawn to—a long, steep descent with rocks to jump off," he says. The year he arrived he opened a snowboard shop in Mammoth Lakes called Wave Rave, which was rated number one on the West Coast several years ago by the SnowSports Industries America (SIA). The shop, not affiliated with the clothing line of the same name (started by an old Boulder friend of his), is now a Mammoth snowboarder hangout. In addition to running the store with his wife, Kim, and traveling to far-flung competitions, Klassen has ridden his board in commercials for Coke, Shell and Visa.

During Mammoth summers he takes his board up into the backcountry and rides the corn until July. Once winter rolls

around again, Klassen can frequently be found on Mammoth Mountain shooting the steep terrain at Paranoid Flats, Dragon's Back, Hemlock Ridge and a rocky part of the summit known as Top of the World. They're perfect places to test his natural freeriding instincts.

"I've always loved going top-to-bottom down things, at high speed, jumping off of everything and being fluid in my line," he says. "That's how I've ridden since I was a little kid. I get off the lift, I know what I want to hit and I go." ◉

"Long, steep descents with rocks to jump off." That's what Steve Klassen came to Mammoth for in 1989.

seasons. With little to be optimistic about, few were willing to make major investments in the town, which stagnated.

In '90-'91, Mammoth Mountain's skier numbers tumbled to only 450,000, and the company was compelled to do something it had never done before. On what has been known ever since as Black Monday, the resort laid off 150 employees in one day, including some who had worked for the mountain for 20 years or longer. It sent such major shock waves through the company and the town, where people had come to count on McCoy's loyalty and generosity, that some still haven't gotten over it more than a decade later.

"It was hard on the company and especially hard on Dave McCoy," Gregory says. "He took tremendous personal financial losses trying to keep the staff that he had developed. We came to a point where we had to [let people go] or we were going to lose the company."

Gregory, a rangy ex-linebacker for the University of Washington Huskies who was briefly with the Kansas City Chiefs, started at Mammoth as a lift operator on Chair 16 in the late '70s and climbed the company ladder. He received an education in the ski area's operations on his way up, working in Mammoth Mountain's lift maintenance and snow removal departments and also as a ski instructor. On the side, Gregory started a heli-ski operation in 1979 that he ran for 10 years, carrying skiers along the Sierra's eastern escarpment from McGee Mountain north past Dunderberg Peak to Sonora Pass above

Above: A soft landing for David Schemenauer in Drop 18.
Below: Acres of frontside cruising for Shane Chandlee.

Bridgeport. By the mid '80s, he had moved up to become Mammoth's personnel officer, a role that expanded to include financial areas of the company when it hit rocky times. He became CEO in 1997.

Looking for creative ways to increase its cash flow, the resort's public relations director, Pam Murphy, came up with the idea of holding a Grateful Dead concert at Mammoth Mountain in the summer of '91. The resort began working out details for a two-day event with rock promoter Bill Graham. However, the cautious Mammoth Town Council, worried about the band's gonzo reputation and projections that it might draw thousands more fans to town than its campgrounds could hold, forced them to cancel the concert. It turned into one of the town's hottest political issues. Pranksters started a campaign supporting a run for town councilman by Dead singer Jerry Garcia. After the next election, all three council members who were up for reelection found themselves out of office.

In a process guided by Gregory, Mammoth Mountain began evolving from the idiosyncratic operation it had always been into a more tightly managed business. "[Black Monday] definitely changed a lot of things here at the company," Gregory says. "From then, the town has seen Mammoth become a lot more business-oriented. We have a very strong financial discipline now. [We] make the hard decisions a little bit every day instead of all at once, which is what happened in 1991." Mammoth Mountain also

installed an extensive snowmaking system in the early '90s, digging a new on-mountain lake to supply water so that it could guarantee a Thanksgiving opening.

As if Mammoth Mountain's executives didn't have enough to worry about, the resort also ran into problems with some of the innovative skier conveyances built for them in the '80s and '90s by Yanek Kunczynski, a Carson City, Nevada-based lift manufacturer. His company, Lift Engineering and Construction, had become one of the largest and most successful in North America building the fixed-grip lifts that were state-of-the-art in the '70s, often labeled with the "Yan" name. McCoy struck up a strong friendship with Kunczynski, a former ski racer from Poland, and liked to brainstorm new engineering concepts with him. "Yan and Dave were apt to sketch things on a napkin in the cafeteria and then go out and build it," Armstrong says. "That design and entrepreneurial 'try something' spirit was in Yan and in Dave, and they did a lot together."

Above: Weather is a frequent phenomenon at the summit. Without it there would be no powder. Below: The double-black Dragon's Tail at the far eastern end of the mountain attracts freerider Jason Moore.

Chair 14, a favorite of those aiming to avoid crowds, runs along the ski area's western boundary near Hemlock Ridge.

One of the revolutionary ideas that McCoy developed with Kunczynski—the winch-cats used today to groom ultra-steep slopes where ordinary snowcats can't travel—literally created a new industry. Gregory adds that many of the perfections in fixed-grip lifts also came from the two innovators' idea sessions. "Over a couple of decades Yanek and Dave designed an awful lot of [what became] standard equipment at ski resorts around the United States. Some of the new ideas with fixed-grip technology—the use of aluminum with some of the running gear, the design of the liner sheaves, the use of digital control drive systems—most of these things were the result of collaboration between Dave and Yan."

When fixed-grip technology was replaced in the industry by the more advanced high-speed detachable lifts, Kunczynski shifted into building them. However, in the '80s and '90s, a series of accidents involving Kunczynski's lifts at different ski resorts in the Western U.S. and Canada resulted in dozens of injuries and several deaths. "As Yan moved into high-speed technology, his systems were not as popular and tended to not perform as well," Gregory says. "[His lifts] had some accidents. It was very controversial. The jury's

Left: Big trees, deep powder, the lure of the Mammoth backcountry.
Skier: Nathan Wallace.

still out about how much of it was Yan['s fault] and how much was the operators'." Kunczynski's company finally settled wrongful death suits out of court for multiple millions of dollars. After his lifts came under increasing scrutiny by safety inspectors who found flaws in the equipment, Lift Engineering and Construction filed for bankruptcy in 1995.

Through all of this, however, McCoy remained loyal to his friend Kunczynski and continued to commission new ski lifts from him in the years before Lift Engineering's bankruptcy. After McCoy acquired June Mountain in the mid 1980s, he engaged Yan to build its new access lift, the "QMC tram," which the pair designed together using fresh new technology in an attempt to solve a problem with heavy winds. In 1994, McCoy hired Kunczynski to build a high-tech monorail People Mover at Mammoth Mountain to shuttle skiers back and forth between the Main Lodge and Canyon Lodge, and collaborated with him on its design.

However, the prototype QMC tram at June needed constant adjustment and maintenance and was prone to frequent breakdowns, and the resort was finally forced to tear the tram out—an enormous financial loss. John Armstrong says, "The fact that we were always buying the prototype sometimes worked against us. It could have been a market advantage. As it turned out, [lifts] broke down frequently, needed a lot of work. The QMC at June was a huge investment, dramatic new technology, and they

Today's leaders at Mammoth. Above: President Dave McCoy with current CEO Rusty Gregory. Below: Senior Vice Presidents Bill Cockroft (left) and Pam Murphy flank mountain mascot, Woolly.

had to cut it out of the ground." Then one March day at Mammoth, a People Mover car carrying a couple of skiers ran off the end of the track and plopped onto the snow. The passengers sustained only minor injuries, but the People Mover never ran again. The resort finally tore it out as well. (Subsequently, Kunczynski built a people mover based on the same engineering concept to carry people between the Bellagio and the Monte Carlo hotels in Las Vegas, which worked well and continued in regular operation for years.) Eventually, Mammoth Mountain replaced many components of the detachable chairlifts that Kunczynski had built, although it kept in operation the older Yan fixed grip lifts that continued to be very dependable. That marked the end of Mammoth Mountain's tradition of pioneering lift technology, at least for the present. "Some of the wonderful technology that was invented here like lifts, these are businesses we're very careful to stay out of today," Gregory says. "Product liability litigation precludes us from doing the kinds of things that I thought were very interesting and fun that Dave let us do."

By the mid '90s, most of Dave McCoy's children had had enough of the ski business. To their father's great disappointment, all of them except Penny decided they wanted to sell their shares in the company. "Dave and Roma and the kids went through a difficult ownership transition," Gregory says. "Dave had a dream of turning his company over to his family. [But] five of the six McCoy children wanted to

do other things." Gregory put together the complicated deal with Intrawest, selling them 33 percent of the company the first year and then additional shares later for a total of 59 percent, but leaving McCoy with 80 percent of the voting control of the company.

Intrawest arrived ready to lay out its vision for refashioning the town and started by building a string of new condos and the Sierra Star golf course before launching into the huge Village at Mammoth project. Once Intrawest started building, Mammoth's sluggish real estate market was suddenly revitalized. Smiling Mammoth homeowners found that their properties had doubled in value in just a few years.

Intrawest vice president Doug Ogilvy says, "Between Intrawest and Mammoth Mountain Ski Area, we spent $300 million in Mammoth [from 1997 to 2002]. That has a ripple effect. Property values are up about a billion dollars since we came to town. You're now finding people building nicer houses, renovating

Above: Open glades, untracked lines. What could be better? Below: Swirling powder in Drop Out Chutes. Skier: Nathan Wallace.

THE SHERWIN SKI AREA

In the 1980s, Mammoth Lakes developer Tom Dempsey decided to pursue his own longtime dream: building a second ski resort at Mammoth. This was the same Tom Dempsey who had helped assemble Mammoth Mountain's Chair 1 in the '50s when he was 19, butting heads with the lead engineer until Dave McCoy came to his support. In the intervening years, Dempsey had become Mammoth's most prominent developer. His company, Dempsey Construction, built major projects in the town, including the extensive Snowcreek Condominiums and a nine-hole golf course in the nearby Mammoth Creek meadow, where the town had originally been seated. He planned to build the Sherwin ski area in the mountains just south of Old Mammoth, on the other side of

Dave McCoy (center), with his son Gary (left) supported the plan of Tom Dempsey (right) to build a new ski area.

town from Mammoth Mountain. The U.S. Forest Service had designated the site as a possible winter sports area as far back as the '60s, and local visionaries had kicked around the idea of building a ski resort in the Sherwins for at least that long.

Dempsey's company drew up plans for a resort with nine lifts (including six high-speed quads) that could carry 8,000 skiers a day up to its mostly intermediate terrain. The ski area would have three ski lodges, parking for 2,000 cars and 30 buses, and 10 miles of access roads. *The Mammoth Times* reported that Dempsey spent eight years and around $1.5 million to prepare the Environmental Impact Statement for the resort. McCoy, who believed the new ski resort would complement his own by providing skiers with another reason to come to town, supported Dempsey's plan. In 1990, Mammoth Mountain public relations director Pam Murphy said, "It'll help spread the business around a little, and as far as we're concerned, the sooner the better."

In the modern era, however, environmental obstacles have made building a new ski resort extremely difficult. Environmentalists did challenge the Sherwin plan, pointing out that the proposed resort lay in the path of a key deer migration corridor. However, in 1990 the Forest Service gave Dempsey the go-ahead to advance in the planning process, and the company appeared to have a good chance of building their resort. The proposed new ski area generated much excitement in Mammoth Lakes. Articles about it appeared in the *Los Angeles Times*, and in the early 1990s, newspapers in Mammoth began reporting that the developer might

The proposed plan for Sherwin Ski Area.

soon break ground on the ski area. "SKIING COULD BEGIN BY WINTER OF '92," a sub-headline in the *Mammoth Times* trumpeted in October 1990.

After that, however, Dempsey Construction turned to other projects and placed the ski resort plan on ice—where it still remains. "Dempsey has a whole lot of [developments] in the West and Hawaii, so my understanding was it was just a matter of priorities in their organization," says Forest Service special projects coordinator Sandy Hogan. Unfortunately, Tom Dempsey died in 2000 without ever realizing his dream. Today, the Dempsey company's executive vice president, Gail Frampton, says that the proposed ski area is in a "standoff" because of the Clinton Administration's ban on new road building in designated forest areas. "Our plans now are to wait out the court rulings on the legitimacy of the Clinton roadless initiative," Frampton says. Two decades after it was proposed, the future of the planned resort remains a question mark, and little is heard about it on the streets of Mammoth Lakes. ❂

Above, left: Intrawest's first development project was Juniper Springs. Right: Construction of the new Village at Mammoth, which will provide the town with a center it has never had, was well underway by summer of 2002.

houses and condos, renovating their stores. There's a lot of optimism and enthusiasm."

Even so, not everyone was happy to see Intrawest come to town. Some, most notably Mono County Supervisor Andrea Mead Lawrence, decried what they referred to as the Aspenization of Mammoth. They warned that the town would become a glitzy place where ordinary working people couldn't afford to live or own a house, as has happened at other ski resort towns. Meanwhile, others in town were only worried that Intrawest might not follow through on its plans fast enough.

"People in Mammoth are notoriously pessimistic," Ogilvy adds. "Nobody actually

Dempsey Construction's Snowcreek project in Mammoth Creek Meadow sits near the site of Old Mammoth.

believed Intrawest was ever going to build the Village at Mammoth. They thought we were going to just talk about it for 10 years. When we started pouring concrete, that got people's attention." Construction of the new village and the gondola to transport people up and down the mountain was well underway by summer of 2002. The new hub, with its shops, restaurants, art gallery, taverns and night clubs, is designed to provide a place where resort visitors can entertain themselves for hours in the daytime or evening—without ever having to get into a car.

The ski area kept McCoy's Mammoth-to-June vision on the back burner while it undertook a thorough overhaul of its on-mountain facilities. Mammoth Mountain replaced some of its chairlifts with new high-speed quad chairs that virtually eliminated lift lines, and replaced the uninspired, slow-moving on-mountain cafeterias with much-improved cafes and restaurants. Those and other changes put Mammoth Mountain back on track again. In 2001, the resort's skier visits were back up over 1.1 million.

To raise that even higher, Mammoth Mountain worked

Opposite: Powder power. Zack Yates in the backcountry beneath Mammoth Crest.

Dragon's Tail off Chair 9 offers double-black diamond sweetness after a storm.

with the town on a plan to expand the runway at the tiny airport so that major airlines could land big jets there. That would open the resort up to new customers across the country and beyond, and cut down its reliance on Southern Californians driving up the highway to Mammoth.

"The community needs it, and it's certainly an important part of the resort plan that we've had for quite some time," Gregory says.

In 2000, the FAA authorized a $28.6 million payment for the airport improvements, but the plan quickly ran into opposition from the Sierra Club and other environmental critics. At press time, it wasn't clear when the airport upgrades might go forward.

In recent years, McCoy has taken on the role of ski industry elder statesman. He has often traveled around the country to advise other ski areas about their operations at no charge when they requested his help, and welcomed ski area representatives from around the world who came to observe how Mammoth Mountain worked. McCoy is a revered figure in skiing. He was inducted into the U.S. National Ski Hall of Fame and the California Tourism Hall of Fame. And he has been the recipient of numerous other awards and honors, including the AT&T Skiing Award, the Ski Business Hall of Fame award, the National Ski Areas Association Lifetime Achievement Award and the U.S. Ski Writers Association Golden Quill Award. In perhaps the

Opposite: Silver Chesak takes the extreme route down Roger's Run.

Not all skiing is on the mountain. Kristi Leskinen does a railslide across a Mammoth Lakes bridge.

finest tribute, in 1994 the California Ski Industry Association began annually awarding the Dave McCoy Achievement Award, which represents "the pioneering spirit, perseverance and inspiration which he has taught so many of us in his years of leadership." In the mid '90s, a local group erected a plaque on the spot at the foot of McGee Mountain where McCoy's old rope tows operated in the 1930s, near some of the remnants of tow machinery that still lie rusting there.

In 2002, 87-year-old McCoy watched his most recent contribution to the town begin to take shape—a new college for Mammoth Lakes. After being asked to aid in the creation of a college, McCoy helped with seed money and worked with his son Gary and other community leaders to create the nonprofit Mammoth Lakes Foundation to establish a campus and performing arts center in the town. That year found Dave McCoy still spending his days behind the desk in his Mammoth Mountain office greeting the steady stream of visitors who stop by to chat, seek his help or advice or just pay tribute. In between guests and well-wishers, McCoy sits and thinks about new ways to make Mammoth Mountain a better place to ski. ✿

Left: The look of the future. Tanner Hall flies above Mammoth's Unbound Terrain Park.

acknowledgments

Special thanks to John Armstrong at Mammoth Mountain for his knowledge and patience, and also to Tim Sanford, Andrea Mead Lawrence and Allan Pietrasanta for theirs. Others who helped in a variety of ways include Rob Simpson, Demila Jenner, Chris Lizza, Ingrid P. Wicken, Wolfgang Lert, Linda Meyers Tikalsky, Jill Kinmont Boothe, Toni Milici, Nancy Tallent Larsen, Heather Johnston, Sandy Hogan, Paul Rudder, Susan Szewczak, Joe Szewczak and Mike Yorkey.

Thanks also to the folks at Mountain Sports Press: Bill Grout, Alan Stark, Scott Kronberg, Michelle Schrantz, Chris Salt and Paul Prince, plus Greg Ditrinco at SKI Magazine and Evelyn Spence at *SKIING* Magazine.

At Mammoth Mountain, thanks to Rusty Gregory, Rob Perlman, Pam Murphy, Joani Lynch, Brad Peatross and Chic Gladding. And finally my thanks to Roma McCoy, Gary McCoy and especially Dave McCoy for his patience, graciousness and for his remarkable story.

—Martin Forstenzer

bibliography

Cadillac Desert by Marc Reisner

Gold, Guns and Ghost Towns by W.A. Chalfant

Gunfighters, Highwaymen and Vigilantes: Violence on the Frontier by Roger McGrath

Mammoth Lakes Sierra edited by Genny Smith

Mountain Dreamers by Robert Frohlich

Mountaineering in the Sierra by Clarence King

Old Mammoth by Adele Reed

Pray for Snow: The History of Skiing in Southern California by Ingrid P. Wicken

Roughing It by Mark Twain

The High Sierra by Ezra Bowen

The Lost Cement Mine by James W.A. Wright

The Other Side of the Mountain by E. G. Valens

Wild by Law by Tom Turner and Clifton Carr

photo editor's notes

There are several people who should be recognized for their outstanding contributions to the photography in this book.

A special thanks to Robin Morning, photo researcher, whose efforts helped bring the history of Mammoth to life.

Thanks to Brad Peatross from Mammoth Mountain for answering all my questions and just being great to work with. To TJ, formerly of Mammoth Mountain, thanks for providing your extensive first-rate photography to this lengthy project.

Thanks to all the photographers, whether you submitted one photo or hundreds. Your love of the Sierras shows in your art.

—Scott Kronberg

index

index